A Visitor's Guide to
THE NATIONAL PARKS
OF ENGLAND AND WALES

A Visitor's Guide to

THE NATIONAL PARKS

OF ENGLAND AND WALES

John Wyatt

First published in Great Britain 1988 by
Webb & Bower (Publishers) Limited
This edition published 1993, produced by
The Promotional Reprint Company Limited,
Exclusively for Fraser Stewart Book Wholesale Ltd,
Abbey Chambers, 4 Highbridge Street,
Waltham Abbey, Essex

Text Copyright © 1988 John Wyatt
Illustrations Copyright © 1988 Webb & Bower (Publishers) Limited
All photographs copyright © Countryside
Commission except those individually credited.
Maps are based upon the Ordnance Survey map.
Countryside Commission Copyright © 1988

ISBN 1 87472 341 9

Printed in China

Contents

Introduction

Most of the landscape of England and Wales bears the heavy marks of many centuries of human settlement and toil. There is no true wilderness left, but there are places where a more formidable environment has imposed its constraints on the activities of man. Here, to survive, he has been forced to come to terms with nature; to co-operate rather than contend. Then, by some subtle alchemy, from that blend of what nature has created and man has only modified, have evolved some sublime and eloquent landscapes. They are so different from the busy towns and cities and lowlands where most of us live. Different in every way; not only in their scenery, but in their climate, their rocks and soil, their animals and plants and the people who make a living from their land.

These special places are also different from each other: the high moors of Dartmoor and Exmoor in the south west; the coast and cliffs of Pembrokeshire, and hills and mountains of Brecon and Snowdonia in Wales; the Peak District, the Yorkshire Dales and the North York Moors high on the spine of England; the inspirational beauty of the Lake District, and the Roman Wall and remote hills of Northumberland. So valuable are these enclaves that they are now protected as national parks. Not, in England and Wales, owned by the nation, but in the nation's special care, so that their treasured qualities are preserved for all time and for all freely to enjoy.

All these places have an unfailing attraction to millions who seek rest and refreshment, a change from the daily routine of home; who need to broaden experience, to enrich the quality of life – to re-create. For, living as most of us do where land has been mauled and restructured and enslaved, there is that ever-present need to seek out what is nearest to the wild, free and natural: the hills and mountains, woodlands and waters. A 'sense of place' is one of feelings. It cannot be rationalised. But the need is quite real and quite basic, and to some of us as vital as food and drink.

It is significant that the first great interest in countryside came during the economic upheaval of the Industrial Revolution when, for the first time in history, more people were living in the towns than on the land. Perhaps deep down in our instincts it is a desire to return home; for a whole population can of necessity leave the countryside, but the countryside will not necessarily leave the population. It is the crucial part of our heritage.

From that early popular desire to appreciate the beauty of the countryside and to enjoy it, came also the first urge to protect it. William Wordsworth, from his Grasmere cottage, saw the hurt being caused by some new-rich who were buying land in the Lake District and putting up pretentious buildings wholly alien to the landscape; and he expressed a hope in his best-selling *Guide to the Lakes* that such people and others should show better care, observing that his views would be shared by many visitors who regarded the Lake District as a 'sort of national property, in which every man has a right and interest who has an eye to perceive and a heart to enjoy'.

There were a growing number whose eyes and hearts were affected by the countryside, and the movement towards 'national properties', later 'national parks', began, not only in this country. The world's first national park was designated at Yellowstone in the United States of America in 1872. In Britain moves came more slowly with the organization of numerous groups and societies with a concern for the countryside. An early move came in 1895 with the founding of The National Trust for Places of Historic Interest or Natural Beauty, which is today known simply as The National Trust.

The drive for national parks with free access to the hills and open country began in earnest between the wars when the desire of more and more people to re-create themselves in unspoilt and protected countryside became urgent. Countryside recreation was no longer seen as a prerogative of a leisured class. Factory and office workers and the unemployed of that time had discovered the freedom of the outdoors which offered extended exercise for the limbs, clean air for the lungs, fair prospects for the eyes and joy for the heart.

Outdoor organizations flourished, and the period saw a rallying and amalgamation of them, spurred by frustration at government inaction. One protest took the form of a mass trespass on part of the Peak District's grouse moors in 1932. A large group of organizations met at Westminster in 1935 and founded the Standing Committee for National Parks to continue the lobbying of parliament. (It exists to this day as the Council for National Parks.) Then the second world war intervened.

The post-war years of reconstruction brought new optimism. The idea of healthy open-air recreation in a green countryside epitomised much that had been fought for on the battlefields.

In 1945 the government of the time received a report from John Dower (the 'Dower Report') which recommended the establishment of national parks, and a new guiding government agency, a National Parks Commission (later to become the Countryside Commission). A Land

Fund was set up from which it was intended the national parks should benefit. The Dower Report, of course, saw that the national parks of England and Wales would have to be different to other national parks in the world. For here the land was privately owned, and the areas had to be protected, not as museums, but as working environments. Here was a new and challenging concept.

Then in 1947 a National Parks Committee, with Sir Arthur Hobhouse as chairman, proposed an administrative system for the parks which was embodied in the National Parks and Access to the Countryside Act of 1949.

The triumph of the campaigners at the long awaited achievement, however, was tempered by bitter disappointment. The Act fell far short of their hopes. Nothing ever came from the Land Fund. The arrangements for the organization of the individual national park authorities were seen by many to be too weak. The first two national parks to be designated, the Peak District and the Lake District, were to be administered by independent boards; but in the later designations these arrangements were not followed through. As a result the new authorities were committees of the county councils; and in those park areas covered by more than one county the control was fragmented. The membership of all park authority boards and committees was to consist of two-thirds of local county and district council nominees and the remaining third were to be ministerial appointees made on the advice of the Countryside Commission.

This arrangement was confirmed by the 1972 Local Government Act, which led to the appointment of national park officers and some better funding, though the low parliamentary priority for countryside conservation is betrayed still by the very minute part of the national budget given to national parks: a mere £13.5 million in 1988, which represents 75 per cent of the parks' normal expenditure from public funds. (The parks do obtain other income, for example from the sale of publications.) However, national park staff are still very thin on the ground; work that could be done is left undone or postponed. It could be said that much of what has been achieved has been in spite of, not because of, governmental attitudes. However, it must be admitted that the agreed funding in the late 1980s has risen above the rate of inflation.

The national parks are charged with two main statutory duties: to preserve and enhance the natural beauty of the area and to help the public to enjoy the amenities; they also have to have due regard to the social and economic well-being of the local communities. To fulfill the first duty the national parks are planning authorities. The evidence of their success is very largely in what is *not* seen. The exercise of planning control has ensured that ugly and intrusive building developments can be prevented. However, planning powers have limitations. Agriculture is largely outside the scope of planning control, though the park authorities have responsibility to comment on applications for Ministry of Agriculture farm grants. Commercial forestry is exempt. Informal

agreements have, however, been made with the Forestry Commission in some national parks to exclude important and sensitive areas from future planting.

The parks have found themselves too often in the role of David against Goliaths. For instance that one giant, the Ministry of Transport, urged on by a rich and powerful road lobby. An 'improved' A66 road in the Lake District was ploughed through the delightful Greta Gorge, and alongside Bassenthwaite Lake in the 1970s, in spite of proposals by the Park Authority and all conservation groups for a less damaging alternative. Again, more recently, in 1987, in Dartmoor National Park, in spite of enormous opposition the Government agreed an A30 by-pass to Okehampton through the northern edge of the park when again there was a good alternative. And how to oppose the giant of the Ministry of Defence? Large tracts of national parks are in its control. In spite of the Hobhouse Committee concept that people 'need the refreshment which is obtainable from the beauty and *quietness* of unspoilt country', the parks are used by Air Force jets to practise horrendously noisy low-level flying.

However, David has had his victories. To quote a few: there was the successful opposition to the construction of a motorway link through the Peak National Park in 1977; to extract potash from the North York Moors National Park in 1979; the plans by British Nuclear Fuels and the North-West Water Authority in the Lake District National Park to extract water from Wast Water and Ennerdale Water, and, most recently, proposals to extend quarrying in both the Peak District and Yorkshire Dales.

Some of the positive work of the park authorities includes help with landscaping schemes and tree planting, the removal of eyesores, the undergrounding of cables, and the restoration of buildings and walls. Practical help is given to hill farmers through 'upland management' schemes. Sensitive areas of moorland, broadleaved woodlands and areas of archaeological and natural history interest have been acquired for their protection, for demonstrating management techniques, or for ensuring public access. Extensive public access agreements have been made with landowners. A tremendous amount of work continues to be done to restore, repair and sign the network of several thousands of miles of footpaths and bridleways. Ranger and warden services are there to manage the amenities and to help the visitors with advice, and they lead guided walks with the parks' information services which have centres throughout their areas, offering published literature, lectures and displays.

Some national parks face a great pressure for new building. Parks are pleasant places to live and more people would like a home in them. This also raises a social problem as property prices are too high for local working people although cottages are sold as holiday homes. Without a viable community, schools and shops may close, creating villages that are open 'only in season'. But there are other grave social issues. High land in national parks is grazing for hill sheep. If farm subsidies are reduced as a response to sheep meat mountains and European Common Market policy, the industry is so marginal that many farms will go. Already hundreds of hill farmers and their families in all the national parks have left the land, while their farms are absorbed into larger, more viable holdings. With reduced manpower on the farms the land cannot be cared for as it once was. The park authorities, with their limited powers, have been trying to ensure that hill farms survive and social structures are maintained.

Should there be more national parks? One of the two areas omitted from the Hobhouse Committee's suggested twelve was the Broads, which is the largest area of freshwater wetlands in Britain, with navigable waterways and attractive reed beds, fens and woodlands of willows and alder. They have long been a source of recreation for boat enthusiasts. With the enactment of the Broads Bill in 1988, a statutory Broads Authority will now be responsible for an area with national park status, even if it is not called a 'national park'.

People spend a total of nearly ninety million days visiting the national parks every year. More people than ever before are concerned about conservation, and membership of conservation societies and outdoor organizations continues to grow. There is a tremendous amount of goodwill. The footpath erosion everywhere is evidence, if it was needed, of the enormous popularity of walking in the countryside. Tourism is a major source of employment in our parks, and a support to the local economy. Maintaining the parks well, in partnership with the local people, is an investment in the future.

The commitment of national park authorities has been beyond question. Patterns have been set. Valuable expertise has been gained in an integrated management that depends on that close working and supportive relationship with the local community; landowners and farmers, the outdoor and conservation organizations, and other statutory authorities with a concern for the countryside.

There are now over a thousand national parks throughout the world. Although the national parks of England and Wales are not, in the internationally accepted definition of national parks, 'wilderness areas', they do come under the international concept of 'protected landscapes', characteristic of the 'harmonious interaction of man and land' while 'providing opportunities for public enjoyment – within the normal lifestyle and economic activities' of the areas. At a time when economic forces, aided by the power of modern technology, are everywhere putting more and more valued countryside under threat, the British system of that integrated management is attracting international interest.

That which speaks to the spirit defies adequate description, and this book can only be a poor introduction to our national parks. The beauty there that the partnership of nature and man has created needs to be seen and felt with the mind unwound of worries and the senses wide open. That different world it offers is only a little journey-time away. It is there to stay.

Dartmoor National Park

Two days before, I had walked Dartmoor's lark-loud heights in sunshine. White clouds chased across a blue sky, and the cool moving air felt like wine. Elation almost gave my feet wings. But now the mood was different. Periodic attacks of wind-thrown rain drove at me malevolently. The sun came and went. When it came, light was livid and lambent on the long wet moor. When it went and the storm clouds shuttered down, the way was so uncertain that I had to fumble with cold fingers to pull out my compass. I found the route point I was seeking, though. It came suddenly. A double row of standing stones stretching to the distance, a tall one at the high end, and as I squelched down the wet slope by the long avenue there was a squat wide one at the other end, like a tombstone, set in an

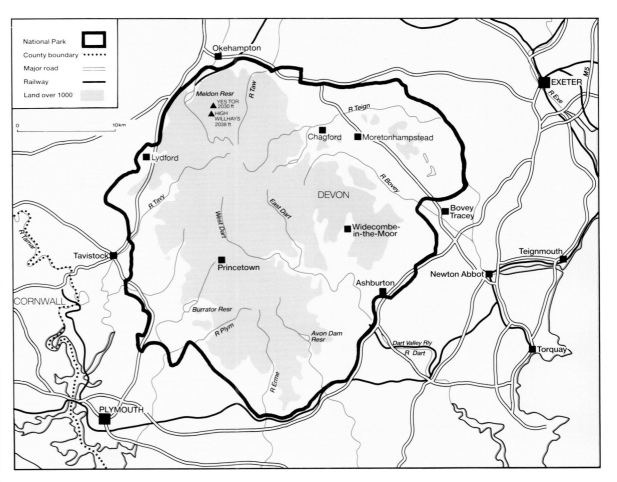

Year of designation	1951
Area	365 sq miles (945 sq km)
	(boundary currently under review)
Population	29,139 (1981)
Land use (approx)	
Enclosed farmland	35%
Open country	52%
Commercial forestry	4.5%
Deciduous woodland	4.5%
Land ownership (approx)	
National Park	1.4%
Forestry Commission	1.8%
Water Authority	3.8%
National Trust	3.7%
Ministry of Defence	14.0%
Natural areas of special interest	
National Nature Reserves	3
Other nature reserves	4
Sites of Special Scientific Interest	28

Administering authority
Dartmoor National Park Authority,
Parke, Haytor Road,
Bovey Tracey,
Newton Abbot,
Devon,
TQ13 9JQ
Tel: (0626) 832093
The national park is wholly within the county of Devon.

Left:
Dartmoor National Park – a high, windswept moor above the rich, warm lands of South Devon.

Dartmoor National Park.

apron of pavement. Changing light with shafts breaking through the racing clouds heightened the mystery. No one knows why, or will ever know why, thousands of years ago the early settlers on the moor built these strange alignments. There are scores of them on Dartmoor with many other ancient remains in a density elsewhere unknown.

I learned in youthful Plymouth days that the moor has two faces. There is the open one with barbarous, challenging, stretching empty distances. And the darkly mysterious one, all questions with no answers. The north-western part of the moor can give a sense of remoteness unmatched in any other place in England.

21

There are some fine examples of the thatcher's art in the park. Some of the villages and town areas are specially protected as 'Conservation areas'.

The air of mystery, if one has the imaginative taste for it, is enhanced by the strange shapes of the tors which crown the peaks. The fragmented columns of granite, distorted by erosion, suggest all sorts of images: utterly ruined Gothic castles and cathedrals, conferences of crouching giants, prehistoric monsters. At close quarters even more grotesque. One can make out ugly faces, and gargoyles of the most fiendish kind. Sections are piled upon sections, some seeming perilously poised.

If solitude is needed, the moorland of Dartmoor National Park offers that solitude chastened by vast perspective. But the park is not all moorland. For that comforting enclosed kind of solitude it is easily possible to be wrapped in trees. There are extensive, unregimented oak woodlands in the valleys and gorges – of the Darts, Teign, Bovey, Webburns and Lyd, with the company of moving water. Wonderful places in the new green of bird-singing spring, or the soul-stirring fire of autumn.

Then, of course, if solitude is not for the mood of the day there are the farmlands with their patterns of walls and hedges, the lanes, the remoter valleys and hamlets with tall-towered churches and many thatched cottages; and the popular places with postcard and gift shops, pubs with log fires, and cream teas. Nothing too vulgar here (but with traffic problems in season).

Essentially, the national park is two high moorland plateaux separated by the upper river reaches of the West and East Dart. To the east of them is a more rolling landscape cleaved by deep river valleys, with woodland, farmland, a network of roads and lanes, and the scattering of settlements.

The high land is on granite. Put simply, 280 million years ago the land of which Dartmoor is now a part consisted of layers of sedimentary rocks. Then came a period of earth movements, the 'Armorican', which raised mountains in Europe, Asia, and eastern America. One effect of this on the south-west

An outlier at Houndtor.

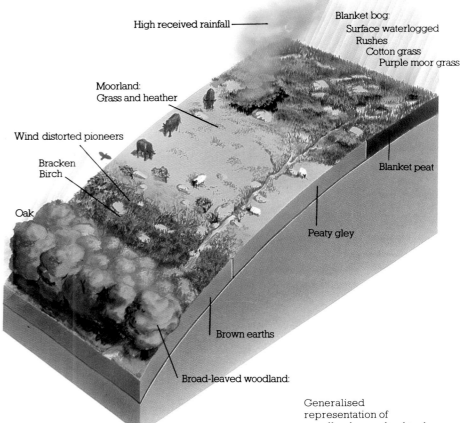

High received rainfall

Blanket bog:
Surface waterlogged
Rushes
Cotton grass
Purple moor grass

Moorland:
Grass and heather

Wind distorted pioneers

Blanket peat

Bracken
Birch

Oak

Peaty gley

Brown earths

Broad-leaved woodland:

of England was an upward movement of molten magma which thrust through the sedimentary rocks to cool slowly under the earth's crust as granite. The present-day exposure of the granite is due to the succeeding millions of years of erosion which took away the surrounding softer rocks. Tors were formed when high bosses of this exposure were broken up by storm and frost.

When this molten magma rose, its tremendous heat baked the surrounding sedimentary rocks through which it was thrust, and super-heated gases and vapours broke through the cracks to condense into veins of crystalline minerals. One of these which greatly influenced the later economics of Dartmoor and Cornwall was 'cassiterite', an oxide of tin. But there were other minerals in various traces including copper, lead and iron. In the south west of the park are very deep beds of china clay (kaolinite) formed from the decomposition of feldspar, one of the principle elements of granite, caused here, it is thought, by super-heated steam.

In succeeding ages severe erosion was followed by inundations of the sea. When the Ice Ages affected Britain the ice sheets did not reach Dartmoor, but accumulating ice and snow, deep

The River Erme in southern Dartmoor. Earth movements tilted the land upwards in the north, hence the southern flow of rivers seen today. Here is Piles Copse, one of the relict oak woodlands.

perma-frost and the later thaw-water, continued the erosion process. As the climate warmed, the land was colonised by forest. However, poor drainage on the upland levels meant that when wetter periods intervened there was soon a dearth of vegetation there and peat beds formed. The forest declined more rapidly with the arrival of man.

Neolithic and Bronze Age colonisation was to become very extensive, up to the highest parts of the moor, and it can be assumed that present-day lowland settlements are built over very ancient ones. Neolithic man built his burial chambers to last, but not his homes, of which there are hardly any signs today. 'Spinsters' Rock' in the north west of the park is a striking remnant of a burial chamber.

The agriculturalists of the Bronze Age brought a

Generalised representation of woodland, moorland and blanket bog continuum. Prehistoric peoples cleared much of the natural woodland cover on high Dartmoor – accidentally by fires and deliberately for agricultural reasons – and in effect moorland has been 'inserted' between the blanket bogs and retreating woodland. The moorland resource has been used almost continuously through the centuries but climatic, ecological and human factors still influence moorland processes.

Tor formation. By 75 million years ago sedimentary rocks were worn away to leave the granite exposed. Weathering eroded the domed outcrops, and freeze-thaw sequences at the Ice Age broke open the rock along its joints. Fallen blocks form the 'clitter' below the bases.

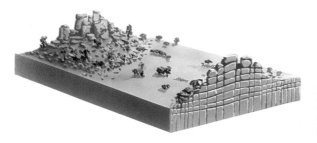

A stone row at Long Ash Hill near Merrivale. There are many double rows like this one. Others are singles and some are trebles.

religious fervour which produced the many stone alignments, the stone circles and the standing stones. Good examples can be seen a little way from the B3357 road on the rise east of Merrivale. Here there are two dual stone alignments, one 596 ft long (182 m) and the other 865 ft (264 m), and nearby is a cist, a fragmented stone circle, and a large standing stone. There are hut circles nearby. The Bronze Age dead – probably only the more important people – were buried under round cairns.

Hut circles show the ring of stones forming the bases of prehistoric dwellings. They are difficult to date, but most about the area are thought to be Bronze Age. Around 2,000 have been identified so far. Groups of huts often stood in a walled enclosure. An obvious example of such settlement remains is at Grimspound, a short walk up from a minor road running south to Widecombe-in-the-Moor from the Moretonhampstead to Two Bridges road. Grimspound was a settlement of pastoralists and these hill farmers also contained their grazing areas within banks of stone and turf. These boundaries, or 'reaves', can hardly be seen at ground level and become more obvious from the air in the right conditions. The banks sometimes stretch for miles.

'Spinsters' Rock'. Said to have been built by two spinsters before breakfast, but actually the remains of a chambered tomb which has lost its covering of earth.

Prehistoric hut circles suggest that the huts consisted of a low stone wall with a crawl-in entrance, sometimes sheltered with a porch. A central pole would have supported other poles interwoven with thinner wood round which was made a steeply-pitched roof of overlapping turfs, possibly thatch, with a smoke hole.

forts are less than a mile apart across the River Teign, at Prestonbury and Cranbrook, with another one at Wooston less than two miles down valley. Cranbrook is a good example with clearly defined ramparts and ditches commanding a grand view of the wooded valley.

The Romans apparently did not establish a presence in the area for no traces of them have been found. It is likely that at that period the population was not large. There is little to see on the ground now until the medieval period is reached. The pattern of settlement which had then emerged was one of lower farming areas using parts of the moor for the summer grazing of their stock. This continued through the centuries. Domesday Book described the manorial system on Dartmoor, and listed some sixty place-names but mentioned only a few towns. One of these was the Saxon town of Lydford to the west of the moor. It is likely that at the time of the Conquest there was considerable new settlement around that area, winning land from the moorland fringe. Domesday Book also mentions the farm of Willsworthy to the south east of Lydford, worked by four slaves for 'Alured the Breton' who apparently in 1066 managed the farm for Siward, a

There was some obvious order in their system but how it was exercised we shall never know.

Another type of settlement was used by arable farmers of the fertile lower land to the south east. This consisted of a small number of rectangular fields surrounded by a wall with three or four huts built by the field sides. For some reason these hut circles are twice as large as those of the pastoralists. An example of this settlement pattern can be seen at Foales Arrishes, one mile south east of Widecombe-in-the-Moor.

It was the coming of a less kind climate that caused the moor dwellers to drift down into the valleys. A combination of woodland destruction, poor land husbandry and wetness eventually produced the agriculturally inhospitable landscape we see today. The surrounding valleys offered more promise and gradually there came new tools to assist them – made of iron.

The 'hill forts' are acknowledged to belong to the Iron Age. Was a defensive structure a response to heightened competition for good land? There are hill forts around the edges of the moorland. One example can be seen in woods at Hembury, on the hill north west of Buckfast above the Dart. Two hill

Grimspound prehistoric enclosure. Great effort was needed to build this circle enclosing 4 acres (1.6 ha) and over twenty huts. The wall would have been 9 ft (2.7 m) thick and around 6 ft (2 m) high. Some of the big stones would need considerable manhandling. The entrance to the south east is paved. No giants built the walls for the hut circles are quite small: between 10 and 15 ft (3–4.5 m) wide.

grasses and moss, can be detected almost anywhere round the moor sides and enclaves. There are also widely distributed signs of old mills and 'blowing houses', for the early crude methods of crushing the ore and smelting were replaced by some thirteenth century milling technology. Remains can be seen, for instance, in the Walkham Valley east of Merrivale, one area a short distance from the road on land where the national park has negotiated access. Here the granite ingot mould and the wheel position can be seen. A later feature of mining activity was the making of 'pillow mounds' to establish rabbit warrens. Rabbits figured high in the miners' diet.

Streaming at last became less productive and was

Saxon. The farm still exists. When the Normans occupied Lydford they built one of the castles now within the park. Further proof of Lydford's ancient standing is the dedication of its church – to St Petroc, a Celtic saint.

The abbey at Buckfast was established before the Conquest. Indeed it has been suggested that the Benedictine monks who settled there in 1018 occupied a Celtic site. Just outside the park pre-Conquest abbeys were built at Tavistock and Buckland. The abbeys had their parts to play in Dartmoor's economy, particularly developing the woollen and cloth industries.

But another important industry began to develop. Tin mining had already prospered in Cornwall, and anciently some tin had been mined in Devon, but prospecting and mining began in earnest in the twelfth century around the granite fringe of Dartmoor. The earliest method of winning the ore was by 'streaming': washing the lighter material away from the heavier metal ore in a flow of water. Streams were often diverted or straightened to get a strong flow. Prospecting ('costearing') and streaming became very widespread and intense, and the heaps of waste, most covered now by

Lydford Castle was built in 1195. The ugly square structure never played a great defensive role but served as a prison in the fierce and cruel enforcement of stannary laws.

A medieval tin mill or 'blowing house'. Leats were cunningly constructed to direct water onto a water-wheel which worked a crusher and pumped the bellows of a small furnace fueled with peat or wood. The molten metal was poured into a stone mould. Remains of a number of these mills have been discovered in many places.

The secret of making good gunpowder is fine milling, and a good supply of charcoal. Water power was used to mill powder south west of Postbridge. The remains of the buildings can be seen, suitably scattered to isolate accidents in the dangerous milling process.

The basis of the agricultural industry however, (probably suffering at periods from interference from the mining industry) was wool. The traditional breed of sheep was White-face. Its wool is tough and hard wearing, too much so alas for modern fashion. It was once used to produce navy serge, for the bulldog breed of mariners needed something tough and lasting. Nowadays the wool is used in

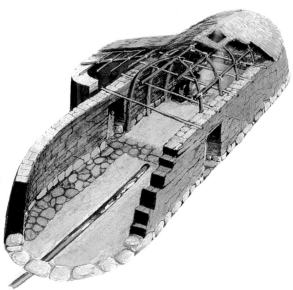

Probable construction of an early medieval longhouse. One end was living room, with cattle housed in the other, sharing the same entrance. A drain had an outlet to a gable wall.

superseded by an 'open cast' method of exploiting lodes in the fourteenth and succeeding centuries. As can be seen, deep gullies were dug into the hillsides and became very extensive. Adits were driven into the hillsides after Tudor times, but mine shafts were not sunk until the nineteenth century, and were never so successful as those of their Cornish neighbours.

From the beginning the mining industry was responsible for the development of 'stannary' towns to which the ingots were taken for assaying and taxing. Ashburton and Chagford within the park were two of these towns, while without were Tavistock and Plympton. Lydford was the administration centre from which the stannary laws were enforced, from all accounts with only summary justice and ferocious cruelty. The gibbet on Gibbet Hill, now a popular viewpoint to the south, probably never lacked occupancy.

When the tin ores ran out, other metal ores were found and mined. In the eighteenth and nineteenth century copper mining particularly brought some prosperity. Lead was mined too. North of Mary Tavy the Wheal Betsy mine was profitable. The ruin of the engine house is preserved by the National Trust.

Dartmoor ponies still roam the moors as they have for centuries, though they no longer go to work in the Welsh coal mines, carry packs, or tin ore, or haul sledges over the rough moorland tracks.

carpets, but it takes dye beautifully and sweaters made of it are attractive and should last a lifetime. Alas White-face are much less popular now as they are not quick maturing; Scotch Black-face and cross breeds are more profitable.

Although hardy cattle have been pastured on the moor since the mid-nineteenth century, the famous Dartmoor ponies have been grazing there from at least the Dark Ages. Below the moor, mixed farming continues as it has done since Saxon times. But, in some areas, settlements have been abandoned due to a number of factors, including worsening weather conditions and the Black Death. The best known hamlet abandoned in the fourteenth century is behind Houndtor. Houndtor itself has to be one of my favourite places; its granite outcrop is so complex in shape. It is a great Gothic symphony in stone. Did the children of the deserted hamlet play here? Or were they told the legend of the black hounds of the night which hide here by day to await the hours of darkness? (The legend probably gave Conan Doyle the idea for *The Hound of the Baskervilles*.) Honeybag Tor, Greator Rocks, and Bowerman's Nose are other grotesque tors none too far away.

Farming on Dartmoor has always had its ups and downs, but in the first half of the nineteenth century, with the improvements in road communications and the innovations of new farming methods, there was some prosperity - more land was taken into production. A large number of the buildings around the park date from that period. Then came the farming decline at the turn of the century which signalled the end to wealthy landowners enclosing areas of moorland under the ancient practice of 'newtaking'. Up to the eighteenth century it was only small farmers, who were tenants of the Ancient Tenements along the Dart river valleys, who were

Building foundations at Houndtor deserted village. The remains of eleven buildings can be traced, three of them 'longhouses' There is no certain way of knowing why the inhabitants left in the fourteenth century. Perhaps it was not suddenly as a result of plague, but brought on by a gradual deterioration of arable growing conditions. Three of the buildings held kilns for drying grain, including oats and rye.

allowed to take over a new area of eight acres of moorland whenever a new tenancy began. Then owners of larger holdings took over some of the Ancient Tenements and, with grants from the Duchy of Cornwall, were encouraged to enclose further areas of moorland, and even some on the borders of Dartmoor, often to the surprise of local residents. The resulting pattern of land ownership on the moor is causing problems to this day; another example of how ancient practices have continued on Dartmoor up to modern times.

Later on better roads, and the coming of the railways, encouraged the establishment of the tourist trade. The hotel trade in Chagford and Yelverton partly developed as a result of the nearby railway stations.

The Dartmoor Preservation Association was

The buzzard, which is often seen in seemingly effortless flight, is Dartmoor's largest bird of prey.

established in 1883 to counter the enclosure of commons threatened by the too rapid changes which came from commercial pressures. What has changed? Thanks to those conservationists and the commendable restraint of the local people, not a great deal for the worse. The establishment as a national park means that the living landscape of Dartmoor is preserved; its archaeological remains, its flora and fauna. 42,000 acres (17,000 ha), 16 per cent of the park, is either in nature reserves or Sites of Special Scientific Interest. 2,500 acres (1,000 ha) of

Tormentil, once used as a herb to cure 'the torments', is everywhere on cropped moorland.

system for regulating the use of the commons. The commons were, and still are, well used by visitors; before the Act this was by let, not by right. Now visitors, subject to certain regulations, have legal access on foot and horseback. The Act created a Dartmoor Commoners' Council with statutory backing for the control of livestock husbandry on the commons. In effect it gives the Park Authority, and the farmers depending upon the common land of Dartmoor, the joint responsibility of stewardship over the commons.

The conservation of the animals and plants on the commons is a major concern. Thirty per cent of the common land is blanket bog above 1,200 ft (366 m), a deep peat area holding a great deal of water. There are areas of heather (for instance north of Postbridge) and this has to be conserved by 'swaling' (burning) at intervals. High blanket bog with cotton grass, sphagnum moss, deer grass and rushes is found in most of the national parks, but the naturalists' interests centre on Dartmoor's position as the southernmost of the national parks with a wet climate but milder average temperature.

There are some superb woodlands in the park

Dartmoor is the only regular breeding site of the dunlin in the south. It is here at its southernmost limit.

woodland are protected by Tree Preservation Orders.

In taking a leading role in conservation the Park Authority has entered into thirty-seven management agreements (1987) to protect habitats and obtain public access. It also holds land itself for conservation and public amenity. The largest freehold ownings are at Holne Moor and Woods, 1,735 acres (702 ha) and around Haytor, 1,089 acres (441 ha). Muscle power in practical conservation tasks is undertaken by the Authority's Upland Management Service and the Rangers, often with assistance from volunteers.

The Park Authority enjoys good relationships with the landowners. The major landowner is the Duke of Cornwall (HRH the Prince of Wales), with 90,000 acres (36,420 ha). 41 per cent of the park is common land on which the area's commoners can exercise certain rights along with the Lords of the Manors and some freehold owners. Previously the commons were regulated by manorial courts, but the courts have long ceased to function. A major step forward in the conservation of the commons came with the achievement by the Park Authority of the Dartmoor Commons Act of 1985 which set up a

Bracken looks attractive in the winter but has spread extensively over the moorland, smothering grazing land.

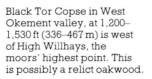

Black Tor Copse in West Okement valley, at 1,200–1,530 ft (336–467 m) is west of High Willhays, the moors' highest point. This is possibly a relict oakwood.

and it is difficult to choose the best. Yarner Wood National Nature Reserve by Bovey Tracey offers good nature trails. Becky Falls, between there and Manaton, offers an excellent piece of woodland managed by the Park Authority with a waterfall (handsome rather than dramatic) for good measure. There is a rich ground flora with ferns and lichens. Are there remnants about Dartmoor of the ancient woodlands? There are probably three. Wistman's Wood, north of Two Bridges, is a possible one. Because of its weird stunted appearance it has been a tourist attraction for over a century.

There is a lot of choice of particularly attractive river sides. For waterfalls one should see Lydford Gorge (National Trust, open April to October). Here again the woodland is very special, with tall-pillared trees racing upwards for the light, with lush ground flora flourishing in the moist atmosphere. The water pours through a narrow cleft to swirl into 'The Devil's Cauldron', and at the southern end there is a long skein of falling water, 'The White Lady'.

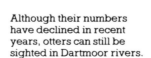

Although their numbers have declined in recent years, otters can still be sighted in Dartmoor rivers.

460 miles (740 km) of public rights of way in the care of the Park's Ranger Service. Then there is the open moor. But there is one serious limitation. The Ministry of Defence has control of some 33,000 acres (13,300 ha) of the highest moorland in the north – the most remote and arguably the most rewarding area

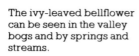

The lovely pearl-bordered fritillary butterfly whose larvae feed on woodland violets.

The ivy-leaved bellflower can be seen in the valley bogs and by springs and streams.

Of old flower-full hay meadows alas there are few. They are alien to modern agricultural methods. The best of the survivors are protected as Sites of Special Scientific Interest or by management agreements.

For walkers, especially those who can read maps, the recreational possibilities are wide. There are

for the walker, including the lovely area in the upper Tavy. But it is not all bad. Access here is allowed on most weekends, and on weekdays in those areas where and when firing is not taking place. Information on what is open and when is displayed at Park information centres, police stations, and post offices. Information on walking routes, and the park's extensive guided walks programme, is available at any of the Park's centres.

There are many handsome hamlets and villages, the best of them protected by the Park Authority as special 'Conservation Areas'. Only a few attractions can be mentioned here. For an exploration of the park there is a choice of touring centres but motorists are warned that many roads are very narrow and they should take note of the colour signing system when planning routes. Moretonhampstead is a very attractive town with seventeenth century almshouses and is one of the best touring centres with access to the through (black) route south westwards through the park's centre. The road goes by Bennet's Cross, one of the crosses and standing stones which are old route markers, and the remotest inn, Warren House, once the miners' hostelry. It has a fire which has never been allowed to go out, it is said, for well over a hundred years. Postbridge is beyond with the best of the clapper bridges, made with huge slabs.

There is a Park visitor centre here. Beyond is Two Bridges. Wistman's Wood is one and a half miles up valley from here – a walk, not an easy stroll.

Princetown is south west again at 1,400 ft (426 m) above sea level and containing the grim prison built in 1806 to house French and American prisoners of war. Since 1850 it has been the notorious convict prison. Princetown is an administrative centre for the Duchy of Cornwall. South westwards again is Burrator Reservoir and by a very narrow road is the exquisite little hamlet of Sheepstor.

Eastwards from Two Bridges is Dartmeet, a beauty spot with another clapper bridge and with woods and ancient monuments around.

Southwards from Moretonhampstead is North Bovey, a pretty seventeenth-century hamlet around a village green, and Manaton, which is similarly disposed and has a photogenic row of thatched buildings near the church. Becky Falls is nearby and a little further a favourite viewpoint: on Trendlebere Down, looking along a two mile stretch of woodland in the delectable Bovey valley. Where else could such a stretch of broadleaved woodland be seen? South west of Manaton is the oddly shaped tor of Bowerman's Nose, and beyond again Houndtor. Then south westwards there is the village made famous by a song: Widecombe. The church is dubbed 'cathedral of the moor'. The fifteenth

Teignhead clapper bridge. The bridges are difficult to date. Some are probably quite ancient. Others may have been built by the miners.

century Old Church House (National Trust) is nearby.

North westwards from Moretonhampstead is Chagford, a stannary town and a great walkers' centre with access to the higher moors. There are several Bronze Age sites to its west including the Scorhill circle, field systems and stone alignments. The town has a chunky-looking early tudor inn, the Three Crowns, thatched of course, and other handsome buildings. Across to the north east are a number of attractions. Castle Drogo (National Trust) was built early this century on the splendid scale to a design by Sir Edwin Lutyens for Julius Drewe. It overlooks the River Teign and is open to the

The village of Widecombe-in-the-Moor with St Pancras church. In this part of the country when times were good the churches were not just expanded outwards – but upwards! The tower is 130 ft (36 m) high. It was built after 1638 when lightning struck the church during a service, causing damage, injury and the loss of four lives. (It was of course the work of the devil. The local inn landlord served a man at the time and was surprised when the ale he drank sizzled as it went down his throat!)

public. Down river is Fingle Bridge, an old hefty three-archer by delightful woodlands.

Continuing anti-clockwise the hamlet of Belstone is another of the best take-off points for high moor walkers. Round again past Okehampton (Park visitor centre and small museum) the stone quarries of Meldon are passed and Meldon Reservoir, from which again there is good moorland access including that to Dartmoor's highest point, High Willhays 2,039 ft (621 m). Following the park

of Mary Tavy has the best surviving ruin of an engine house.

Wheeling eastwards, clockwise from Moretonhampstead, Lustleigh is another thatched-cottage-strawberries-and-cream hamlet. Bovey Tracey is outside the park, but south west of it a road climbs by Haytor, a compulsive and rewarding viewpoint. Rippon Tor is to its south west. Buckland-in-the-Moor, southwards, is another of those hamlets making profit for Kodak and Agfa. Down the Dart by lovely woodland is New Bridge (information centre) with its fifteenth century bridge still in situ.

Ashburton is the park's largest settlement (population 2,200), another of the four stannary

Buckfast Abbey. In 1018 it was a Benedictine abbey. It was under the Savigny Order after the Conquest, and in 1147 became a Cistercian. It was ruinous after the Dissolution and the stones were later used to build a Gothic-style mansion in 1805. In 1882 the estate was sold to French Benedictines who built the essential part of the present abbey between 1906 and 1932. The abbey is famed for its honey and tonic wine – on sale to all pilgrims.

boundary south past Lydford there is the church of St Michael's de Rupe, on Brentor. This is one of those strange sites which suggest to some (certainly to me) a deliberate placing over a pagan shrine. East of Brentor, Wheal Betsy mine (National Trust) north

Scorhill stone circle in a wild and beautiful setting above the North Teign.

St Michael's, Brentor. Puzzle: why should a church be built high on a rock, the only access for the heavy building material up a very rough scramble? It could be considered an act of penance to get to the church! It is recorded that in gales the parson (and presumably the congregation) had to approach and leave the church on all fours! Ancient earth works surround the site.

towns, unspoilt and with some notable old buildings dating back to the seventeenth century. Buckfast to the south west is of course the home of the abbey, in lovely surroundings.

Nearby Buckfastleigh was once a woollen manufacturing centre. The churchyard contains an old tomb where are laid the bones of a reputedly wicked man, Sir Richard Cubell. The elaborate structure is to pin him firmly down, for, 'tis said, at his death black hounds (from Houndtor?) raced across the moor to howl over his corpse.

West again and there is the wild southern

moorland; walkers' country. There is good access from Shipley Bridge south west of Buckfastleigh, from whence Brent Moor is soon reached with its carpet of bilberry, shining red in autumn; a delectable place to be. South by Ugborough Moor there are stone rows scattered about ending with one 1,250 ft (381 m) long from Butterdon Hill. But over the top at Erme Plain is a most extraordinary sight: a long line of stones stretching for two miles (3.4 km) from Green Hill in the north to a ring cairn by Stall Moor to the south. The longest alignment anywhere.

So back to the mystery. The man who lives and works close to the land, through the seasons with their rounds of birth, life and death, knows that if it is to provide for his well being, it demands his working co-operation. But there is also a mystical part which speaks to his mind and spirit. We might call early Dartmoor man's response to it superstition: those puzzling patterns of standing stones. But their strangely moving statement is as much a part of the Dartmoor scene as the wide moors themselves, the wooded valleys, the thatched buildings, and those shattered tors. The final effect, of what nature and the hand and spirit of man has made of Dartmoor, is sublime. As a national park at last the partnership is fostered with great care.

A view of Haytor from Greator Rocks.

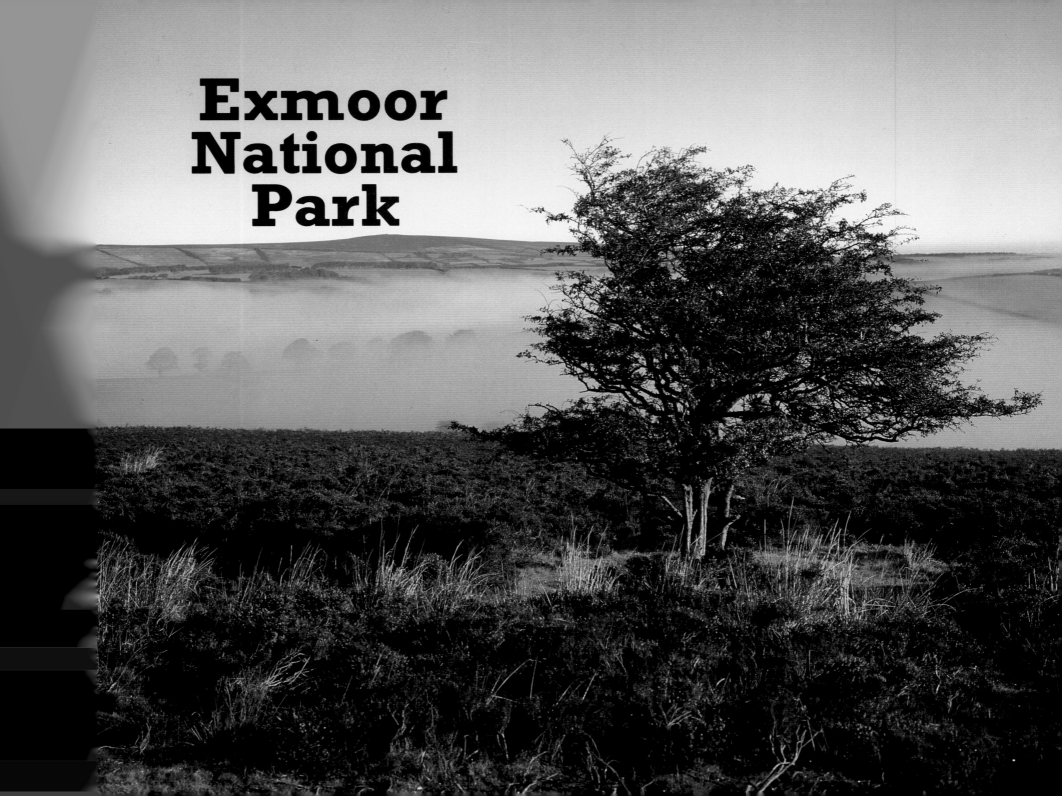

Exmoor National Park

It was a disappointing day. A sunny day had been forecast, but not the fog – but it was certainly there. When I reached Wheddon Cross and looked up I had an idea. There was a light up above the fog. Climbing then to Dunkery Beacon, the highest point on Exmoor, I was right; as I gained height the fog thinned and the light intensified. I was suddenly in glorious golden sunshine on the aromatic heather moor. How can one describe such an experience! As I climbed towards the beacon the lower land below was completely covered in a pure white blanket of cloud rippled with gold. Dunkery Beacon was an island. As I reached the conical mound on the summit itself there was a peacock butterfly. Had it been lurking there, or had it, too, risen to escape the fog? The silence was tangible, heavy, for the world was wrapped around and muted in cotton wool. Only one strange evocative sound – that measured moan of the despairing foghorn, ten miles away along the coast.

Year of designation	1954
Area	265 sq miles (686 sq km)
Population	9,994 (1981)
Land use (approx)	
Enclosed farmland	57%
Open country	28.5%
Commercial forestry	5%
Deciduous woodland	5%
Land ownership (approx)	
National Park	4.3%
Forestry Commission	2%
Water Authority	0.6%
National Trust	10%
Natural areas of special interest	
National Nature Reserves	nil
Other nature reserves	2
Sites of Special Scientific Interest	6

Administering authority

Exmoor National Park Department (Somerset County Council),
Exmoor House,
Dulverton,
Somerset
TA22 9HL
Tel: (0398) 23665
The national park is mainly in the county of Somerset and partly in the county of Devon.

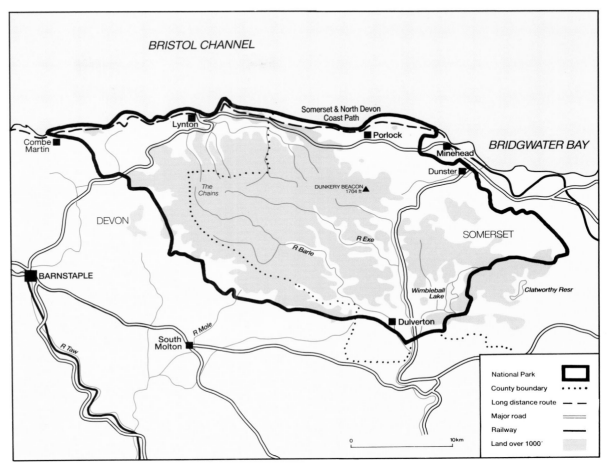

Exmoor National Park.

Left:
Exmoor National Park – a great, beautiful, rolling upland country.

That is one experience of Exmoor; that great beautiful rolling upland country gouged with extraordinarily deep combes, their sides covered in an eye-pleasing mixture of old woodland, and those high cliffs dipping headlong to the sea.

In this landscape in 1797 S T Coleridge and William Wordsworth, both fanatical walkers, trudged many miles over the moors and coastal paths, talking poetry and politics and social problems. And it was here and then that they conceived and composed the Lyrical Ballads in 'the real language of men' and liberated the Romantic period in English poetry.

Was Coleridge, when he dreamt into existence

The coastline is the highest in England, sometimes over a thousand feet (300 m); but the land profile as it dips to the sea is generally 'upturned pudding basin' shape, sloping gradually from the heights, but steepening at the base. The spectacular cliffs are where the coast is exposed to the eroding westerly storms, notably those at Great Hangman at the western end of the park where the cliff has a fall of 800 ft (244 m).

The bones of the landscape are mainly Devonian sandstones and slates of various types, the oldest lying in the north and the youngest in the south. The flow of the Ice Age which honed and carved away most of Britain had lost momentum on a line from the Bristol Channel to the Thames so Exmoor shows no dramatic effect of glaciation. The natural terracing feature on some of the hills was caused by landslips during alternate periods of freeze and thaw.

With the moderating climate after the Ice Age came the plants, first those of the tundra, followed by pioneer trees such as birch and pine. Then the colonisation became much more varied. Oak woods with elms and an understorey of hazel spread over the whole area. And the animals came, including those red deer herds for which Exmoor is famous.

'Valley of Rocks' near Lynton. Here isolated rocks of slate and sandstone set in clay were probably left at a glacial margin.

Kubla Khan, in a farmhouse near Porlock after taking opium, exaggerating his mental image of one of those deep tree-clad combes:

'And here were forests ancient as the hills
Enfolding sunny spots of greenery.
But o that deep romantic chasm which slanted
Down the green hill athwart a cedarn cover!
A savage place –'

Here, too, he wrote *The Ancient Mariner*, surely from images of ships sailing for Bristol, seen from the coastal headlands where his hermit lived:

'The hermit good lives in that wood
Which slopes down to the sea –'

Exmoor National Park, in Somerset and North Devon, is largely an upland area, higher at its northern end facing the sea. The major part of this land mass is plateau, cleft by deep valleys – the combes – typically with steep sides covered in woodland and giving shelter to farms, villages and road routes. However, on the east of the park the Brendon Hills are not as high, with no wide plateau, and are more rolling.

The slopes of South Barton Wood with the River Barle.

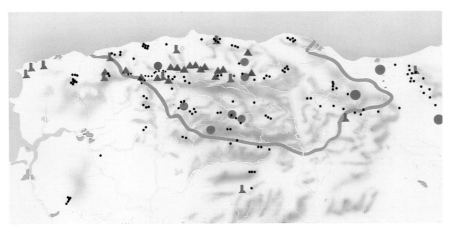

- ● Stone circle
- ▲ Stone setting
- ⊥ Standing stone
- . Round barrow
- ● Bell barrow
- ● Disc barrow
- ● Bronze implement hoard
- ╱ National Park boundary

Signs of early settlement.

It was not until the Bronze Age, around 2000 BC, that man began to make his mark on the Exmoor landscape. The forest started to be cleared, the lower land farmed, the higher grazed. There are many burial mounds and stone circles from this period. A survey has revealed that there could be more than 2,000 sites or groupings. None of the examples are spectacular, though there are standing stones, notably at Longstone Barrow, at about 1,500 ft (457 m) on the western end of the wild moor known as The Chains.

The Bronze Age was superseded by the Iron Age. It is likely that there were new settlers at that time, but not necessarily invaders. It is thought that the hill forts date from the Iron Age period. There is one such on the heights of Shoulsbarrow Common at the western end of the park. By the time of the Roman occupation the inhabitants could be called 'Celts' of the legendary Dumnonii tribe. The Romans must have found the land too rough to be worth much interest, and the inhabitants no real threat, as there are few signs of Roman occupation even though it became very extensive to the east and on the other side of the Bristol channel. The inhabitants of south Wales were troublesome though, as evidenced by the number of road networks and forts there, and it was probably to keep an eye on that coast, and over

the Bristol Channel used by Irish pirates, that the Romans had at least two watch points and signalling towers on the Exmoor coast: one near Martinhoe west of Lynton, and one at Old Barrow to the east.

When the Romans withdrew their forces the coast was wide open for more settlement. The first visitors were Christian missionaries from Wales and Ireland. There are many legends about these first saints. St Dubricius (Welsh name Dyffrig), to whom Porlock's church is dedicated, was a scholar of the sixth century and was said to be a friend of King

Arthur, and married him to Guinevere. St Brendon, nick-named 'the navigator', gave his name to Brendon village and its church, strangely situated two and a half miles away from the village. (Was his navigation faulty?) He was an Irish scholar, and was reputed to have come across an island on his travels, celebrated mass on it only to discover afterwards that the 'island' was the back of a basking whale! He was also said to have discovered America!

The Anglo-Saxon settlers probably found the area sparsely populated and chose the easier land on the sides of the valleys for their farms, felling any woods. At that time the Moor became a Royal Forest,

The Caratacus Stone near Spire Cross, Winsford Hill. It has stood here for over 1,400 years. Its Latin inscription is probably sixth century. But it may have been here from the time of the Bronze Age.

held by the Saxon kings. During the Middle Ages the forest laws were strict and a severe hindrance to farming. They were enforced by wardens, verderers, woodwards and foresters; some probably with doubtful credentials. The penalties were fines or confiscations. The men of Devon paid King John 5,000 marks, a huge fortune, to disaforest the county; but they exempted the difficult farming country of Dartmoor and Exmoor.

Exmoor Forest remained crown land through the centuries, dwindling to 10,000 acres (4,047 ha) after inclosures, and in 1818 the Crown Commissioners put it up for sale. The successful bid of £50,000 came from a John Knight, a Worcester man who had made a fortune as an ironmaster. He could not see why the grasslands of the moor could not be more profitable. He established farmsteads and let them to tenants who were willing to work hard and convert more land to arable, and improve the rest for stock rearing. Some of these farms still make an important contribution to the economy of the moor to this day. Others failed. The work was continued by his son Frederic, who built several farms, including one at Larkbarrow. However, in the 1840s Larkbarrow was one of the failures. The ruined buildings and surrounding land are now in the ownership of the National Park Authority. It is worth a visit. Strange how an abandoned settlement increases a feeling of solitude.

Exmoor's first appeal is the moor itself. Much of it is heather moorland and best seen in late summer when the moors are deep purple with bloom. Other parts are extensively grassed, the predominant species being purple moor grass which grows well on peaty, even poorly drained, land. On a very clear day among the heather on Dunkery Beacon's 1,704 ft (519 m) summit, looking over the lovely hills and combes below, one can see Dartmoor and North Cornwall to the south-west, while northwards, over the Severn, South Wales is clearly seen, and north-east are glimpses of the Malvern Hills. It is said that when the beacon was lit it could pass on the signal from the heights of Plymouth to Malvern. (Probably in less time than getting a telephone connection today?) The moors are well served with consistently signed public rights of way, offering a host of viewpoints and opportunities to find peace and quiet; and never all that far from a public road.

Everyone of course expects to see the Exmoor ponies. They are not strictly 'wild', but they are allowed to run free. Ponies have roamed the area

Exmoor ponies. Note distinctive light markings around muzzle and eyes.

since before human settlement, and the Exmoor breed can manage on very rough grazing. Their strong jawbones have adapted to this. The breed also has to survive the sometimes harsh winters, and for this the pony has two coats; a very dense undercoat, and a long hairy outer which effectively turns the wet. The pony is brown or dun coloured, light grey around the muzzle and eyes. It stands around twelve hands, but is exceptionally strong for its size and can carry a rider with ease. Because of this it has always been popular. Are these the descendants of those ancient wild ponies? It seems likely. From such small breeds the Celts bred ponies to pull their war chariots. They painted the animals and embellished them with elaborate metal trappings, such as those found in a hoard only an easy pony ride away at Polden Hill near Glastonbury. These hardy beasts, able to cover rough country, were also used by the Celts for their cavalry, which proved such a problem to the Romans. And, later, did King Arthur's cavalry use them against the Saxons?

If excitement is as appealing as peace, then one must go where the moor meets the sea. The park has 29 miles (47 km) of coastline, and the South West

valley sides and the coast are the areas now where the main growth can be seen. Some of the woodlands are protected as Sites of Special Scientific Interest. There is an illusion, as one travels the roads, that the broadleaved woodlands are more extensive than they actually are, for often the views are obscured on either side by high banks topped with tall beeches. In some places it is like travelling through a tunnel; but a great sight in autumn with the sun lighting the reds and golds. In fact, though, only five per cent of the park is woodland in the real sense; and another five per cent in the commercial, conifer sense. The Park Authority has a concern for the conservation of the remaining broadleaved woodlands, and tries to come to an agreement with woodland owners, and encourage the renewal of woodland crafts. Until early this century most of the woods were coppiced, the growth being consistently cared for as an important resource. The coppice wood had many uses. Much of it went to produce charcoal for the iron industry, but it also provided timber for shipbuilding and rural industries. The bark was often stripped and sent to the tanneries where it was boiled and used for the leather curing process. Now

A 'tunnel' of old hedge beech trees covers a minor road.

Peninsula Coast Path offers a feast of adventure. The path follows a meandering way from Minehead in the east to the park's boundary at Combe Martin Bay. There are scores of viewpoints. Foreland Point is one. From Countisbury looking dizzily down to Lynmouth is another. Along the North Walk from Lynton to the Valley of Rocks, along a terrace 400 ft (122 m) above the sea on the cliff face, with a fantastic airy view all the way is yet another. Can it be real? Then on to the climb of Castle Rock, easily accomplished. The floor of the Valley of Rocks was probably once the course of the River Lyn which later broke a barrier down to Lynmouth. Here one can wonder at the strange formations: Chimney Rock, Rugged Jack, and the Devil's Cheesewring where, Lorna Doone readers will remember, Mother Meldrum found shelter in winter. There are more eye-feasts along the coast; past the Roman signal point and beacon by Martinhoe, and notably at Great Hangman, then Little Hangman and down by Lester Cliff to the rock-girt bay of Combe Martin.

Arguably none of the original forest cover is left, for all the existing woods have probably regenerated after being cleared at some time. Steep slopes, impractical for farming purposes, on the

From Countisbury Hill. Lynton is in the background with Lynmouth below.

many of the woods are unmanaged. If grazing animals are allowed in to them no new seedlings can survive. Some woods are threatened by alien species, particularly rhododendron, which if unchecked can smother all regeneration. Others are threatened more seriously by commercialism. In purely economic terms it pays to fell the old woods and replant with quick-growing alien spruce trees. This has to be prevented; 6,000 acres (2,428 ha) of woodland have been listed for their landscape value. The Park Authority has used its limited powers to place conservation orders on some 700 acres (283 ha), and the Somerset County Council has also acquired threatened woodland so that 1,000 acres (405 ha) are now within the care of the Park. Luckily some 2,000 more acres (809 ha) are safe in the hands of the National Trust.

Woods are vital to the Exmoor scene. Descending from Dunkery Hill to Luccombe, the view of the woods of the Holnicote Estate is a delight. There are, too, the ancient woodlands on the sides of the East Lyn river as it descends steeply to Watersmeet (National Trust) and Lynmouth. Watersmeet is a popular beauty spot, and the walk to it from Lynmouth is very fine all the way. Falling water

Dunster Castle. Medieval but restored in the nineteenth century when the grounds were planted with exotic trees. Owned by the Luttrell family for six centuries it is now in the care of the National Trust.

Woodlands line the reaches of the East Lyn.

amid trees can never fail to please. Another lovely walk is up from Porlock through Hawk Combe and Homebush Woods. And all the way along the coastal strip from Porlock westwards to Glenthorne are 6 miles (9.7 km) of lovely old woodland. At Glenthorne there is a pinetum with very large specimen conifers. There are some beautiful woodlands too (not particularly old) on the walk up from Selworthy to Selworthy Beacon (National Trust), with watercress in the stream to add spice to a picnic. Similarly, in the valley of the River Heddon, around Hunters Inn. The walk from Dulverton 9 miles (14.5 km) north-westwards, by the ancient clapper bridge of Tarr Steps, to Withypool goes through mixed woodland nearly all the way.

Some of the wealthy landowners of the nineteenth century planted exotic trees in their parks which are now mature and very fine. We are in their debt. Some good examples are to be seen in the grounds of Dunster Castle (National Trust).

Are the famous red deer of Exmoor residents of the woods or of the moor? Properly they are animals of open woodland, but their great strength is in their adaptability. The red deer is Britain's largest wild land animal. The stag will stand at

The head of a mature red deer stag.

seen almost anywhere – on the moor or in the rose bed of someone's garden! The fallow and the Sika on Exmoor are escapees from private deer parks. The fallow deer is smaller than the red and is a grazing rather than a browsing animal. Its antlers are palmate. The Sika prefers woodland glades; a native of Japan it looks rather like a small red deer.

Farming has had to adapt to the very varied and contrasting terrain. Arable farming is only possible in the lower alluvial soils, such as that running east from Porlock, and the north side of the Brendon Hills. At Combe Martin there are market gardens on the south-facing slopes, and Professor Hoskins in *The Making of the English Landscape* points out that the field patterns there show evidence of the 'strip' systems of the Anglo-Saxon open field methods, accentuated by later plantings of boundary hedges. This can be seen as Combe Martin is approached by the minor road to the south-west from Berry Down.

The farming scene, because of its adaptations, is British countryside at its best, with hedges, trees and walls. No great spread or ranches here. Beech hedges are a feature of the higher land and mainly date from the nineteenth century Enclosure Acts. Where hedges have become redundant, neglected

around 4 ft (1.2 m) at the shoulder and can weigh around 20 stone (127 kilo). It grows new antlers each year, dropping them in April when they are pushed out by the new growth. The size and number of points on the antlers each year increase with age. It uses the array to fend off rival stags approaching its gathered harem of hinds, who are hornless. The rutting season is in mid autumn. The stags rarely hurt themselves seriously in the fights. It is more of a rattling, pushing match. During this time the stag makes its characteristic challenging roar ('belling'). It is an eerie sound often answered by a distant rival. It is rather odd to hear it on a still night while standing in a street in urban Minehead.

The best time to observe the deer is at early morning or late evening, but a great deal of luck is required as the herds wander about and are soon alerted by human scent. Their camouflage is good too and they are easily missed.

There are three other deer species in the park: the roe, the fallow, and the Sika. Of these the small and very pretty roe is the only native species. It stands about 2 ft 4 in (.7 m) at the shoulder and the buck has distinct erect antlers, not a spread. The roe is a shy woodland creature, but wanders and can be

A high field of oats. Normally arable farming is only possible in the deep soils of the alluvial plains.

and allowed to grow on, their twists, bends and reachings add to the scene. Some of those by the ruins of Larkbarrow look like prehistoric monsters. In places old hedges have been thinned out and the beeches allowed to grow into fine specimens. The result is a pleasing colonnade, or an avenue.

Boundary walls are usually built from flat stones and slates laid vertically, diagonally, or in the 'herring-bone' pattern. There is a splendid example of the vertical type in the boundary wall of Brendon church. Those laid horizontally betray the fact that the Knight family brought shepherds in from the north, for this is the northern method. No doubt it was thought that the northern men would know how to care for stock on the harsh landscape of the moor. The stock is a mixture of breeds, some of them brought from the north. It is pleasant to see belted Galloway cattle when that breed is getting scarcer in Galloway itself.

The human population of the national park is less than 10,000 and there are only five small towns. The popular holiday resorts of Minehead and Combe Martin lie just outside the boundaries. There is a scattering of small, extremely attractive and neatly kept villages to reward the explorer.

A redundant beech hedge grows on to produce a very attractive and typical feature.

The village church at Exford.

Of the five towns, Dunster is one of those not-to-be-missed picture villages with a distinct stamp of the medieval: cobbled ways, old cottages, some of them thatched, a very fine priory church, wide high street with seventeenth century octagonal yarn market, packhorse bridge, working water mill and castle. Its attractions are, alas, too popular at times and are somewhat obscured by parked cars throughout the holiday season. Some of the shops, though little altered in appearance, cater for the tourist trade.

Dulverton is a pleasant little country town at the southern edge of the park. The old work-house there now houses the workers of the National Park Authority. It is their headquarters and main Information Centre. There is good walking in the area.

Lynton and Lynmouth are more than neighbours; the former is the upper storey of the latter, the former being atop the cliff, the latter at sea-shore bottom. The two are connected for pedestrians with a most ingenious nineteenth century, 900 foot (274 m) cliff railway, which runs entirely on water power on a very simple system. Lynton is an unashamed holiday resort of the engaging Victorian

Roadwater village sheltered in the Washford river valley below the Brendon Hills.

Below left:
The attractive harbour town and resort of Lynmouth.

Below:
Exmoor House. Once a Poor Law Institution, now the headquarters and Information Centre of the National Park Authority.

The Park owes much to the concern of many property owners for conservation. Here a cottage at Selworthy Green is being re-thatched.

kind. Lynmouth is an attractive little harbour, which is also connected to the east by the viciously steep A39 road. In 1952 the moor had unprecedented deluges of rain for several days. Funneled down the steeps of East and West Lyn rivers a wall of water hit Lynmouth. Buildings and houses were destroyed and there was loss of life. Rebuilding has healed the scars but the memories remain.

Porlock is another old village of charm in a lovely setting. The little harbour and beach are two miles away at Porlock Weir.

Exmoor National Park was designated to preserve the landscape for the public to enjoy for all time. Its Authority has successfully seen that all building is in keeping with the area. However the main threat to the landscape has been on the Moor itself, and the Park Authority has lacked the powers to prevent some of it. Subsidies from the Ministry of Agriculture for land improvement have persuaded some landowners to plough, drain, and fertilise areas of moorland, and between 1947 and 1976 some 11,000 acres (4,450 ha) had been lost. Since then, in the face of public concern, the Park Authority has successfully negotiated management agreements with farmers and landowners; and with

The small harbour of Porlock Weir.

A craftsman employed by the National Park making a gate.

Visitors receiving advice at the Park Information Centre at Combe Martin.

the help of special government 'grants has paid compensation where it could be shown that the agreements would bring financial disadvantages. The Park Authority has also found it necessary to acquire some 5,500 acres (2,225 ha) of moorland for its protection. Luckily, too, the National Trust owns a tenth of the national park, and having the same conservation objectives as the Park Authority, co-operates closely. In the fluid situation of EEC farming policies the future is uncertain; but at least the Park Authority has secured the advantage of some good sympathetic working relationships with landowners and farmers, and the need to conserve the moor has achieved some political acceptance.

On the practical side of helping the public to enjoy and appreciate the park, the Authority has done a splendid job in signing and caring for the 600 miles (966 km) of public rights of way; a standard which should be the envy of most other footpath authorities. They also successfully deal with a litter problem which is an irritating feature of the British countryside. The eyes and ears of the Park Authority are the working rangers, who assist visitors and residents with advice and practical help. The Information Service provides centres with literature and maps, and organises guided walks and talks.

A tourism development action plan devised by the Authority has resulted in the provision of many full-time jobs. Now that tourism is the major

industry, the numbers employed are greater than those in agriculture.

Exmoor is a model of how such a varied and precious landscape can be conserved for the benefit of all, and the Authority has done some valuable pioneering work. If Coleridge could return to the Moor he would find little change from when he walked it. He could still write, as he did in 1798 about his evening walk home across Exmoor to Nether Stowey in the Quantocks:

'The light has left the summit of the hill,
Though still a sunny gleam lies beautiful,
Aslant the ivied beacon. Now farewell,
Farewell, awhile, o soft and silent spot!
On the green sheep-track, up the heathy hill
Homeward I wend my way; and lo! recalled
From bodings that have well-nigh wearied me,
I find myself upon the brow, and pause
Startled! And after lonely sojourning
In such a quiet and surrounding nook,
This burst of prospect, here the shadowy main,
Dim-tinted, there the mighty majesty
Of that huge amphitheatre of rich
And elmy fields –'

One can still be startled and delighted by the prospects of moor and sea and fields, now and in the future. For this is a National Park – Exmoor.

Brecon Beacons National Park

There is nothing quite like the Brecon Beacons mountain range anywhere else in Britain. Its form is extraordinary. The Beacons hang over the valley of the Usk like great ruddy petrified waves, with the crests at some moment just before the break. They look untamed, yet not as savage as their northern countrymen. The Snowdonia mountains grab your attention and throw their challenge. The Brecon Beacons, and their lusty neighbours the Black Mountains to the east, and Fforest Fawr and Black Mountain to the west, have a strange wild dignity.

But more years ago than I care to remember, my first approach to this delightful country was from the other end altogether, and to a completely different landscape, for the mountains dip to the south with their tails in limestone country, and our guide led us to the waterfalls. Anyone who knows the area will

Year of designation	1957
Area	519 sq miles (1,344 sq km)
Population	32,170 (1981)
Land use (approx)	
Enclosed farmland	43%
Open country	41%
Commercial forestry	9%
Deciduous woodland	4%
Land ownership (approx)	
National Park	13%
Forestry Commission	8%
Water authority	4%
National Trust	3%
Ministry of Defence	0.1%
Natural areas of special interest	
National Nature Reserves	5
Other nature reserves	2 local and 17 others
Sites of Special Scientific Interest	57

Administering authority
Brecon Beacons National Park Authority,
7 Glamorgan Street,
Brecon,
Powys,
LD3 7DP
Tel: (0874) 4437
The national park is mainly within the county of Powys, with areas within the counties of Dyfed, Gwent and Mid-Glamorgan.

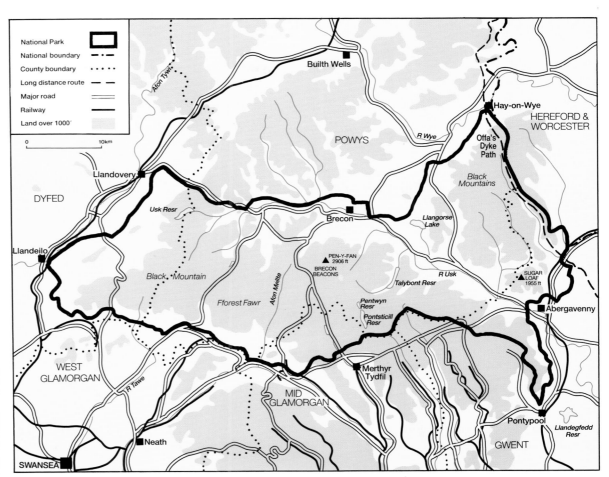

Left:
Brecon Beacons National Park. The high country of South Wales gives a glorious sense of space.

not be surprised that the visit was memorable. Every national park has its cascades, and some are superb. But there is surely nothing to match the tight area of falls on the back end of the southern watershed of Fforest Fawr, down the wooded sides of the Neath and the Mellte, and their tributaries, Afon Pyrddin and Afon Hepste. We walked in early spring sunshine from Pontneddfechan up onto the airy limestone cliff of Craig y Ddinas over the gorge of the Mellte, then walked through the trees by the muffled sounds of falling water and reached Sgwd yr Eira, hearing its roar before we saw it, for it had rained hard and long. The fall was not high, not more than twenty-five feet – but it spoke! When

Brecon Beacons National Park.

A view from Pen y Fan, the highest point in Brecon Beacons National Park.

Mountains. The Black Mountains' northern escarpment faces the Wye valley. A number of river valleys score their way from the heights to the south-east. Waun Fach, 2,660 ft (811 m) is the highest peak. The Sugar Loaf, 1,955 ft (598 m), is at the southern end.

The awesome northern sandstone cliffs of the Beacons show the horizontal stripes of the bedding planes. The highest point is Pen y Fan, 2,907 ft (886 m) and is shouldered by its near brothers, Corn Du to the west and Cribyn to the east.

To the west the range falls to the Storey Arms, the highest point on the A470 road at 1,440 ft (439 m), and the far side rises to the Fforest Fawr range with its highest point, at 2,409 ft (734 m) soon reached. Three other peaks separated by deep valleys spread over eight miles, and then beyond another cross-moor road, the A4067, rise the Black Mountain range. (Here it must be explained that the Black Mountain (singular) to the west should not be confused with the Black Mountains (plural) to the east.) A line of cliffs in the Black Mountain range face east, rising to 2,630 ft (802 m) above the little lake of Lyn y Fan Fawr, then north and west above Llyn y Fan Fach. The southern slopes are as wild and

Sgwd Clun-gwyn, one of the waterfalls on the Mellte.

nature's voice is muted it can be passed unnoticed. But when it grips you hard by the ears there is no escape. We were led across the torrent, not by any bridge, but on the wide easy path behind the falls, behind an opaline wall of booming water in strangely rushing vaporous air currents.

I remember less, from the excitement at that time, the scrambling and sliding wet walk up the gorge of the Mellte to view the three other falls. The impressive wide one in the middle I now know to have the delicious name of Sgwd Isaf Clun-gwyn. (Every name sings like poetry here.) But where the river swept out of sight through the dark cavern of Porth yr Ogof – that looked like the portal of hell and it haunted my dreams.

But this of course was limestone and millstone grit country. Brecon Beacons National Park covers a sprawl of the southern mountains of Wales, and also the beautiful green swelling landscape of river-curving valleys. The river Usk with its splendid trout pools and rapids rises on the north side of Black Mountain, flows eastwards by the park's northern boundary by Brecon town, being joined by Afon Tarell, then flows south-eastwards separating the Brecon Beacons from the Black

remote as any solitude-seeker would wish.

Apart from an area of older Ordovician and Silurian rocks to the north-west, the rocks of the higher land are mainly Devonian sandstones; 'Brownstone' with carboniferous limestones and millstone grits to the south. The whole has been uplifted east to west by the Armorican earth movements, with the high points to the north, dipping to the south. Cracks and faults were opened by the movement.

During the Ice Ages the area was affected by glaciation. The north-facing cliffs and cwms (hollows) are classical features, for on this side away

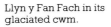

from the warmth of the sun, snow and ice lingered. Below Pen y Fan on the Beacons the little lake of Llyn Cwm Llwch is retained at the bottom of a cwm scooped out by descending ice and dammed by the glacial debris (moraines). Llyn y Fan Fawr and Llyn y Fan Fach below the Black Mountain were similarly formed. Llangorse Lake (Llyn Syfaddan), the largest natural lake, was also trapped by moraines in a hollow. Another effect of glaciation which can be seen are the obviously deeply cut U-shaped valleys.

The lush Senni valley below the austere heights of Fforest Fawr.

Ystradfellte's 'Waterfall Country'.

Llyn y Fan Fach in its glaciated cwm.

The limestone country to the south shows all the classical features. Water absorbs carbon dioxide to make a weak acid solution which reacts with, and dissolves, limestone. So there are 'limestone pavements', sheets of rock with water-worn fissures (grikes). There are numerous swallow holes (sink holes or shake holes) where the surface water has 'eaten' its way below ground, and then there are underground watercourses and caverns. The park is therefore a major caving area of Britain, the concentrations of caves being in the higher valleys of the Neath, the Mellte and the Tawe, as well as at Mynydd Llangattock, south of Crickhowell.

A popular caving area is around the Craig-y-nos Country Park in the Tawe valley. Dan-yr-ogof is the best known cave. The Ogof Ffynnon-ddu to the east, because of the area's high geological importance, is a National Nature Reserve. Another cave in a National Nature Reserve, Agen Allwedd at Craig y Cilau, south-west of Llangattock, has around fourteen miles of passages. Access is permitted for experienced parties only.

South of the limestone is an area of coarse sandstone, the millstone grit, before the coal fields

Left:
One of the spectacular swallow holes is Cwm Pwll y Rhyd in the upper Neath. In dry weather no water reaches it, but in overflow conditions in the higher fissures water spills over a shelf to disappear for a time in its gape.

A reconstruction of the excavated Gwernvale long cairn. In the wider end an indented forecourt might suggest an entrance, but in fact the passages to the burial chambers were in the sides. It is suggested that the forecourt was probably used for ceremonies, a tribal shrine, or for holding a funeral feast, but the reason for the elaborate structure remains a mystery.

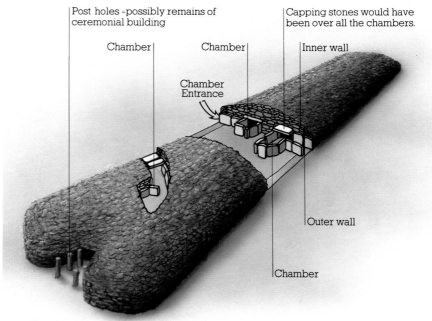

Post holes -possibly remains of ceremonial building

Capping stones would have been over all the chambers.

Chamber

Chamber

Inner wall

Chamber Entrance

Outer wall

Chamber

of South Wales are reached. The grits form those shelves and hollows over-spilled by the waterfalls.

Limestone caves were ready-made homes for early inhabitants who lived by hunting; at Dan-yr-ogof the bone cave (Ogof y Esgyrn) was inhabited by man in Bronze Age and Roman times. As in most of the national parks the first human signs were left by Neolithic farmers, although there is some evidence that Mesolithic hunter/gatherers lived there around 6000 BC. The early farmers made clearances in the forest which was then extensive, cultivated wheat and barley, and kept cattle and pigs. They buried their notable dead under earth mounds, 'long barrows', and later in megalithic tombs. In one kind of tomb prevalent in Wales and the West Country chambers were built of stone slabs with entrance passageways, and the whole was then covered under long trapezoidal mounds much larger than the chambers. Over the thousands of years since their building the coverings of the long cairns have often wasted away, but sometimes they leave their stone chambers standing as 'cromlechs'. There are few examples in the park, but one, Ty Illtud, lies east of the A40 and south-east of Brecon. Another, Ty Isaf, is east of the A479 about three miles south of Talgarth (on private land but visible from the lane). A third remnant is at Gwernvale, just west of Crickhowell.

The late Neolithic Age merged into the Bronze Age culture around 2000 BC when metal tools were at last available to farmers. Evidence shows that in this period the high land was well occupied. It is likely that the farmers lived in wooden structures, which leave little obvious trace of their whereabouts, although archaeologists are finding some signs of settlement. Their graves, however, are more enduring. From this period onwards for at least 2000 years the important dead were buried under round cairns, sometimes as cremations. There are virtually hundreds of cairn remains in the park, often on the heights.

But the more obvious and puzzling remains of Bronze Age activity are in the standing stones, stone rows and circles. There are no spectacular circles here, and one must be careful for small circles could be wasted remains of cairns or later buildings. A circle can be seen north of Craig-y-nos on the west side of the minor road to Glasfynydd Forest. There are two east of Y Pigwn Roman camp. Saith Maen, west of Craig-y-nos, is a stone alignment and there are around thirty standing stones in the park,

A winter scene. Blaen-y-glyn waterfall above Talybont Forest.

51

mainly around the Tawe and the Vale of Usk.

By 600 BC the area had entered the Iron Age. A settlement at Llangorse Lake suggests similarities with the better known prehistoric lake settlements built at Glastonbury and Meare around 150 BC; including the building of an artificial island or 'crannog' onto which huts were built. These lake settlements also occur typically in Ireland and Scotland. One attraction no doubt was the year-round supply of fish. A dug-out canoe dating from AD 800 was dredged from the lake mud in 1925.

Hill forts date from the Iron Age and there are around a score of them in the park. Garn Goch on the north side of Black Mountain is one of the largest in Wales. Apart from the exhilarating views it offers, the quantity of stone in the ruins suggests an impressive picture of walls originally massive in width and height. Crug Hywel above Crickhowell, and Pen-y-crug covering five acres north-west of Brecon, are two other fort remains giving excellent views. Castell Dinas, high on the side of the Black Mountains south-east of Talgarth, was the site of another fort, later built over with a Norman tower.

When the Romans invaded, the people who occupied the area, and the hill forts, were the notoriously warlike Silures. Caratacus had his headquarters here when Ostorius Scapula made the first attempts to invade the area around AD 47. But it was left to Julius Frontinus to take control after AD 74, building the roads commanded by the forts. The main fortress base was at Caerleon (*Isca*) east of present-day Newport, and a road ran from there north-westwards via Usk (*Burrium*) and Abergavenny (*Gobannium*) following the Usk valley

Maen Madoc, a standing stone with a Roman memorial inscription, stands by Sarn Helen Roman road. The name 'Sarn Helen' occurs elsewhere in Wales on Roman roads. One unlikely theory is that it was named after the Welsh wife of Emperor Magnus Maximus. Another is that it comes from 'lleng', Welsh for 'legion'.

to the fort at Y Gaer (*Cicucium*) just west of present-day Brecon. (The remains of the fort are in a farm field about three miles west of Brecon.) This fort was of strategic importance as it commanded a vital crossroads. The westward road from it was important as it went via Llandovery (*Alabum*) to the Roman gold mines at Dolaucothi. Roughly half way between the forts at Brecon and Llandovery it obviously proved necessary to have a large defensive camp, at Y Pigwn, the signs of which can still be seen. Another road ran westwards south of this to an unknown destination. A road ran south-westwards to Neath via Coelbren. This road, Sarn Helen, can still be traced as it crosses the remote terrain on Fforest Fawr. It makes a glorious walk on a fine day. Another road ran southwards from Y Gaer via Penydarren and Merthyr Tydfil and, it can be assumed, to Cardiff. Another ran northwards to Castel Collen, Llandrindod.

After the Romans left in the fifth century the area of the park was in the Welsh princedom of Brycheiniog. ('Brecknock', and 'Breconshire' are Anglicized versions of the name.) The Dark Ages saw activity from both Celtic Christian missionaries and Saxon invaders. The Saxons left the extraordinary late eighth century earthworks of Offa's Dyke, some 168 miles (270 km) long. It was built by King Offa to separate his kingdom of Mercia from the 'Walas', the 'foreigners' of Wales. It was very likely an agreed frontier, hardly a line of defence. The dyke is now obscure in places but a splendid long-distance footpath follows as near as practicable to the original line and part of it runs along much of the park's eastern boundary.

When the Normans spread their occupation of Britain, Brecon town again became a power base for the control of Brycheiniog, but that was not until the 1080s when a force under Bernard de Neufmarché, a half-brother of William the Conqueror, moved into the area from Hay-on-Wye. It is probable that he found Saxon settlements on the best land in the valleys, and the uplands occupied by the old pastoral tribes. The first strategy was to throw up 'motte and bailey' defensive points; earth mounds surrounded by a ditch and surmounted by a palisade around timber buildings. These sites were later abandoned for accommodation in more permanent structures of stone, or a stone building was put upon the motte. Abandoned motte and bailey sites can be found in several places in the park, for instance Trecastle's mound, now partly

system on the native Celts. After the military victory which secured Brycheiniog, probably as a thanksgiving gesture, Bernard de Neufmarché founded a monastery at Brecon, as a Benedictine daughter abbey to the monastery at Battle, Sussex. Its church, St John the Evangelist, survived the Dissolution and became a cathedral to a new diocese in 1923. Its interior is a surprise and a delight. Its thirteenth century origins (built after one or two earlier false starts) can be seen in spite of intervening years of restoration. For instance, the tower and transepts are of the period, and the choir and chancel, though the vaulting is nineteenth century by Sir Gilbert Scott. The nave is fourteenth century and its north and south aisles, once separated from it, were craft-guild chapels. The east end of the north aisle was the corvizors' (shoe-makers) chapel. The south transept was the 'Chapel of the Red-haired Men'; a puzzle, probably referring to the men of the Norman garrison. Among the many interesting features are the Norman font and the very large cresset stone, used for lighting the church. It holds thirty cups.

Also rewarding a visit are the remains of the magnificent Llanthony Priory (a shortening of

Carreg Cennen castle dates from the twelfth century replacing an earlier tower occupied by the princes of Wales. The essential well for the castle is below it and approached by a part built, part excavated passageway.

hidden under trees. The first more permanent castles were usually rectangular towers, later replaced if necessary by round towers. In the case of Brecon's castle, partly built by stones 'quarried' from the Roman fort, there is little left to see. It was deliberately dismantled during the Civil War. The Castle Hotel has been blended into the ruin. Hay's original castle replacing the motte and bailey was built in the twelfth century by a notorious Norman tyrant, William de Breos. It was sacked by Owain Glyndwr in the early fifteenth century, repaired some years later, and then much later its ruin was used to build a house. At Tretower a round tower was built in the late eleventh century on the motte, which had to receive a revetment of stone to take the weight. 'Picard's Tower' now remains an unusual sight. From a distance it looks like a child's broken toy. Standing beneath and looking up, it is a very respectable monument to the Norman's stern will. But undoubtedly the superb gem of the castle ruins is Carreg Cennen east of Llandeilo, crowning a limestone crag with sheer 300 foot cliffs on three sides. It has fantastic views of the surrounding countryside.

The Normans imposed their Roman church

The round tower at Tretower stands uncertainly still on the old motte.

'Llandewi nant Honddu' – 'St David's chapel by the River Honddu') under the Black Mountains. An Augustinian foundation, it was built by the Norman William de Lacey early in the twelfth century. It is said that when he was out hunting he came by chance upon a beautiful chapel dedicated to the Celtic St David. He was instantly converted and resolved to replace it with a religious house. Not long after its building it was abandoned during one of the rebellions and the 'black canons' fled to Gloucester to found a sister house. Rebuilding took place when peace was restored in the late twelfth/early thirteenth centuries and it prospered for a time. But there was further damage and harassment in later rebellions and its wealth was never restored. In the eighteenth century the south tower was converted into a shooting box and now this and the prior's lodge form part of an hotel. The priory gatehouse is now used as a local farmer's barn. However much of the church ruins remain, with the sacristy and part of the chapter house, and it is still an evocative place.

The years following the Norman settlement were often uneasy ones fired by the Welsh urge for independence. The rulers responded with a heavy hand. Brecon town was walled, and only the local English were given lawful standing in it. The upland Welsh were kept at arm's length. Some of the Norman-built churches had fortified towers. Fforest Fawr was a 'royal forest' reserved as a hunting ground for the king, though its status was later allowed to lapse. The situation remained until the Welsh Tudors came to the throne and there was independence. But no great wealth was here. The Welsh noblemen lorded it at the English court and some of the homeland holdings were neglected. Poor road communication encouraged an isolation. Under the Acts of Union of 1536 and 1542, however, Brecon town was chosen as a favoured 'capital' and grew as a market town.

The South Wales economy was boosted tremendously by the coming of the Industrial Revolution and the exploitation of the coalfields lying above the mountains' millstone grits. Though there was a population drift from the rural population southwards, it had surprisingly little effect on the area now covered by the park. Its semi-natural environment remained unspoilt.

The mountain plateaux, surprisingly flattened south of the escarpments, owing to their capping of harder rocks, have the same general natural

The country of the open moors.

Part of the ruins of Llanthony Priory.

characteristics as those in the other national parks. Their acidic soils and harsh climatic conditions and the heavy grazing in many places, reduce the covering to mat grass and sheep's fescue, varying with heather moorland and bilberry and the spreading bracken. Heath bedstraw and tormentil are among the short grasses and in the wet sphagnum, rushes, cotton grass, and purple moor grass. From a farmer's point of view the uplands are not greatly productive but are still pasture for sheep, as they have been through many centuries.

Their aesthetic effect though is a delight – a warped and sinuous green country in summer, tawny and brown in winter, ever changing in the varied light and shadow. The eye-appeal though is not just in the seasonal colours, but in their rare effect on the landscape's sleek looking texture. Its subtlety would elude the greatest artists.

These high lands are haunted by the ravens. They are ranged by buzzards, and one might have the rare viewing of a red kite. At lower levels among the grasses and heather the high-flying larks nest, and the 'parachuting' meadow pipits. The craggy outcrops and old quarry holes are the home of the ring ouzel.

There are some scarce alpine plants where calcareous minerals contained in some of the brownstone layers enrich the soil. Purple saxifrage, the roseroot, and the moss campion are among the alpines found. But of great interest to botanists is not just the discovery of individual species, but of the unique mixtures here of the plant communities – woodland and meadow plants out of their usual habitats and growing among the alpines, and in the mountain gullies and cwms.

The cliffs of Craig Cerrig-gleisiad at the north-eastern spur of Fforest Fawr are protected in a National Nature Reserve for their floristic interest.

Purple saxifrage.

Ley's whitebeam.

There are two extremely rare species – both trees – which grow only in the park and nowhere else. Ley's Whitebeam (*Sorbus leyana*) is protected in a Forest Nature Reserve close to the uninteresting conifer forest of Penmoelallt, and *Sorbus minima* can be found on Mynydd Llangattock.

It is the southern limestone area which offers most to the botanist. Ogof Ffynnon-ddu by Craig-y-nos Country Park is a National Nature Reserve because of its limestone caves, but there are also interesting limestone plant communities on the surface. Caves of course are habitats for bats and there are several species. The lesser horseshoe bat is reported to have colonised areas down to three miles underground.

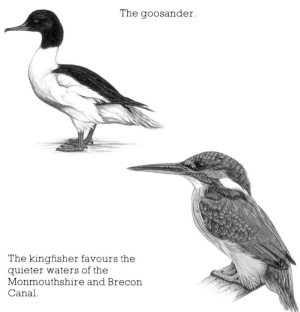

The goosander.

The kingfisher favours the quieter waters of the Monmouthshire and Brecon Canal.

Walking country above Talybont forest.

Old oak woodland in the upper River Tawe area.

For waterfowl, ornithologists could make useful visits to Llangorse Lake in winter. It is too busy with recreational use to be of interest at other times, though the reed warbler is here at its western limit. Among the more common winter visitors are the whooper swans, though not as common as they once were, and goosanders, goldeneye and widgeon. The rivers Wye and Usk are of course well known to anglers.

Of the rarer animals the otter is present, though still scarce. The polecat, almost now exclusive to Wales, thrives. Information on nature reserves can be obtained from the Nature Conservancy Council, or ask at the Park's information centres at Brecon, Abergavenny or Llandovery, or the Park's friendly Mountain Centre, south-west of Brecon, from the A470 west of Libanus. If study in depth is wanted there are courses at the Park's Danywenallt Study Centre.

The Park's staff will also give advice on walking. There is so much to offer. Under the watchful eye of the warden service there are the hundreds of miles of footpaths offering a great variety of easy or testing walks. Then there are the open hills requiring in their negotiation no rough scrambling; and the exhilarating ridge walks. The weather needs to be right and a word of warning is

The polecat.

with its scattering of pleasing settlements; Crickhowell with its medieval stone bridge of thirteen arches, and nearby, across the river, the Monmouthshire and Brecon canal offers level towpath walks. Then there are the sublime Mellte and Neath valleys and the high across-the-moor roads.

Of the neat little towns and villages there is no space here to make mention. But Hay-on-Wye needs one. It is a handsome little town, but if bibliophiles call here they might see little of the national park, for every building, (the whole town and even the castle), seems to be one huge book shop.

The ideal holiday town of Brecon itself has its cathedral, castle ruin, Brecknock Museum, and Christ College school founded by Henry VIII; and in the town of narrow erratic streets there are other elegant Georgian buildings. But over all the silent Beacons rear their heads, reducing the centuries of human affairs to proper proportions.

necessary. One cannot here, as in Snowdonia or the Lake District, easily find shelter from an outcrop during a sudden storm. The heights are wide open and can be potentially hazardous. Apart from the main ridges there are other hills to explore, for instance in the south-east the Sugar Loaf, Ysgyryd Fawr and the Blorenge, and Pen Cerrig-calch, the highest limestone peak.

The waterfalls' attractions have been mentioned. The Forestry Commission offers walking routes, car parks and picnic areas among their conifers. The broadleaved woodlands are in small scattered patches covering only 4 per cent of the park area, and there is a need to recover the sad losses of years past – and those of not all that long ago. The Park Authority is doing its utmost. It has been involved (1988) in some 500 schemes to help landowners plant and manage hardwoods, and has itself an annual planting programme of thousands of trees.

The scattering of trees are an essential part of the serene beauty of the valleys. What is there to match the lovely valley of the Honddu? It even moved the stern William de Lacey to build Llanthony Priory. Then there is the long and varied valley of the Usk

Above Talybont reservoir. Broadleaved trees in the foreground, typical straight lines of the conifer plantations behind. The forests were mainly planted in the 1930s, 50s, and 60s and cover 8 per cent of the parks' area. A landscape strategy map agreed with the Forestry Commission includes restrictions on further plantings, as well as agreeing areas where broadleaved tree planting might be encouraged.

Pembrokeshire Coast National Park

To stride along the cliff top is to have all senses under an exhilarating assault. Below, the sight of the inrolling, restless sea, and the sound of it rushing, pounding and breaking at the base of the rocks. And the salt-smell. And underfoot great sheets of colour: blue and pink, and yellow and white. Subtle scents: thrift, bluebells, gorse and vetch and cowslips, sea campion and red campion, stroked by the wind. Headland after flower-covered headland along the cliff-top miles. And outwards the islands and stacks, white-ringed with surf.

Sometimes it is barbarous. There is no rest in it. It is too dynamic. Perhaps then to find a moment of peace, an opportune descent is needed below the rock walls and the wheeling sea-birds to the soft sand of a secluded strand. In calmer moods its

Year of designation	1952
Area	225 sq miles (583 sq km)
	(boundary under review)
Population	21,531 (1981)
Land use (approx)	
Enclosed farmland	84%
Open country	12%
Commercial forestry	3%
Deciduous woodland	1%
Land ownership (approx)	
National Park	.5%
Forestry Commission	1.2%
National Trust	4.7%
Nature Conservancy Council	.5%
Ministry of Defence	4.5%
Natural areas of special interest	
National Nature Reserves	3
Other nature reserves	21
Sites of Special Scientific Interest	48
Administering authority	

Pembrokeshire Coast National Park Committee (Dyfed County Council), County Offices, Haverfordwest, Pembrokeshire, Dyfed, SA61 1QZ Tel: (0437) 4591 The national park is wholly within the county of Dyfed.

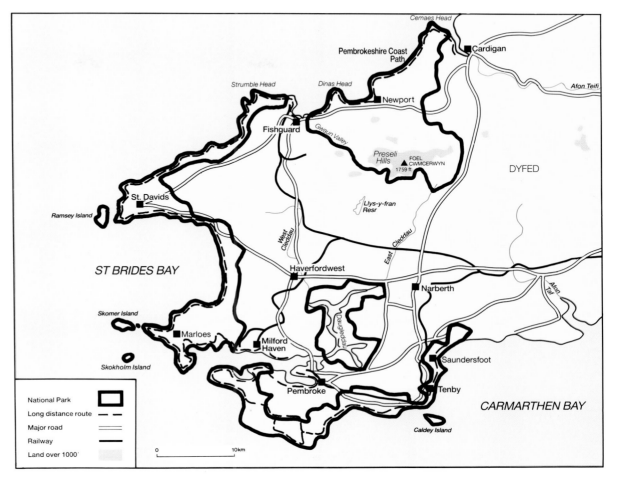

Left:
Pembrokeshire Coast National Park, where the Atlantic breaks on some of Britain's most spectacular coastline.

rhythms must find those sympathetic chords. At those times it is like music.

This is what the Pembrokeshire Coast National Park is to me. It is where spring comes early, autumn is reluctant to leave, and winter's visit is so brief it has no time to make itself at home. Pembrokeshire's gift of mild weather flows from the Gulf Stream. But from the same compass can come a wild fury of a wind that incites the sea to join it in an assault on the cliff bastions. A process that has been grinding on since this earth's beginning. The scene, all along the coast, is all about the formidable erosive powers of the wind and sea.

The coastal strips and the islands famed for their

Pembrokeshire Coast National Park.

was lifted a number of times by earth movements. This has resulted in the 'stepped' appearance of the plateau.

The Preseli Hills rise impressively above these comparative levels. The rocks are Ordovician with igneous outcrops. The outcrop of dolerite here, a hard rock formed from lava cooled just below the earth surface, provided the 'blue stones' which were anciently transported all the long way to Stonehenge.

At the Daugleddau a number of rivers converge to Milford Haven. The rivers were drainage channels during the Ice Ages, and their courses were 'drowned' when sea levels rose following the ice melt. By contrast with the rugged coast this is a more sheltered area of delightfully complex winding creeks and mudflats and 'hanging' woodlands, some of them quite ancient. The streams from the Preseli Hills running westwards feed Afon Gwaun, a river running through hanging woods to Fishguard, and the scenic Afon Nyfer which reaches the sea at Newport. The whole park is a naturalist's paradise, eighteen per cent of it listed as Sites of Special Scientific Interest. An exploration could occupy one for a whole lifetime. And the National

beauty, and their nesting sea-birds are a main feature of this, the smallest of the national parks in the south-west extremity of Wales. But there are also contrasts. There are the wooded valleys of the Daugleddau and the Gwaun. And behind the coast a plateau, 200–300 ft in height (60–90 m) with some rounded hills, eventually rising in steps to a height of 1,760 ft (536 m) on the moors of the Preseli Hills.

Geologically the rocks represent a huge time span from pre-Cambrian to Carboniferous. In the north-west of the park between St David's Head and Strumble Head are spectacular headlands formed of Ordovician igneous rocks, where the seas have bitten into the softer sedimentaries of the bays. By contrast in the south-east, the coast south and westwards from Saundersfoot offers a variety of rocks: dark coal measures, mountain limestone, a warm red sandstone. At Saundersfoot can be seen a much visited exposed geological feature – an anticline, a severe folding of the rocks. In fact severe folding is a geological feature of the whole area and can be seen in many cliff faces. In other circumstances this would produce a folded landscape, but the whole land has been subjected to sea erosion, and it was once a sea bed. The level

Red campion and bluebells bloom around Skomer's bays.

Elegug Stacks are home for razorbills, guillemots, fulmars, kittiwakes and gulls.

Park Authority plays its active part in conserving these varied habitats.

The cliffs and islands are of international importance for their colonies of breeding birds. The red sandstone island of Skokholm, home to the oldest bird observatory in Britain, became well known when Ronald Lockley lived there among 80,000 birds to make his long study before writing the natural history classic *The Island* in 1969. The island has large colonies of puffins and Manx shearwaters, but there are also razorbills, and the mysterious storm petrels as well as the ubiquitous gull species. The island's neighbour, Skomer, is similarly populated. Elegug Stacks are home to

Razorbill.

The Daugleddau, a complexity of mudflats and creeks.

the breeding grounds of the grey seal. Sea watchers might also spot dolphin, porpoise, occasionally basking sharks and whales, although binoculars are needed for closer observation.

All this is exciting enough. But what can one say about the flowers? It is not the rarities which are the attraction but the sheer colourful profusion of maritime, meadow, and heath blooms. There are the uncommon species. The habitat on the stacks is enjoyed by the pink-flowered tree mallow. The deep-yellow Tenby daffodils, though once commoner (before being greatly robbed) are still found in a few places round Tenby. Wavy St John's wort, and the long-leaved sundew are found in some wet areas. The limestone cliffs and plateaux offer real attractions to the exploring botanist. The lovely blue of the spiked speedwell is one favourite of mine. The bright yellow broom on some cliff tops is an unusual prostrate species, an adaptation to the

The Tenby daffodil, a distinctive dwarf species still to be found in old cottage gardens and some hedgerows.

Whitesands Bay, one of the many beaches.

thousands of razorbills (the razorbill is the emblem of the national park) guillemots and puffins. Way out, seven miles (11 km) to the west of Skomer is the island of Grassholm, which is claimed by some 22,000 pairs of gannets – the high divers – a spectacular favourite of coastal birdwatchers.

Apart from the gulls, fulmars and kittiwakes nest on the cliffs. The rare chough has also found a niche in places, enabling it to survive here, although it was once common elsewhere in the UK. Inland the mudflats, and the man-made Bosherston Lily Pools, attract waders and waterfowl in season, Skomer and Ramsey islands and the less accessible beaches are

The grey, or Atlantic, seal. Some of the largest breeding grounds for this seal in Britain are on the Pembrokeshire coast.

Pentre Ifan. The enormous capstone is over 16 ft long by 8 ft, and 2½ ft thick, supported by uprights between 7 and 8 ft high. The original stone chamber was covered by a 'long cairn', about 130 ft (40 m) long. Stones now mark its extent.

salt winds. Typical and uncommon maritime species are also found in the sand dunes. Deciduous woodland covers only one per cent of the park and the Park Authority has been acquiring areas of woodland for its protection. They are also, with management agreements, planting parcels of land that are no longer needed for agriculture.

Agriculture, behind the coastal fringe, is fairly intensive. Some of the country's earliest potatoes are lifted here. Cereals are also grown and there is dairy farming, stock raising and sheep on the Preseli Hills.

It was not the good soil and the climate, though, which attracted the earliest human settlers, but the fishing and hunting. There is evidence of cave occupation over great stretches of time, probably from around 10,000 BC at Little Hoyle Cave and Hoyles Mouth near Tenby, and Nanna's Cave on Caldey Island. Excavations of the cave floors have revealed Stone Age tools among the bones of extinct animals.

The Mesolithic settlers arrived from around 8000 BC. There is some evidence of their occupation as their flint spear and arrow-heads, harpoons and knives have been found. Indeed, archaeologists have discovered a 'chipping' floor near Nab Head which indicates that there was a sizeable flint factory at the time. Perhaps they had trade links with other areas? Much more apparent are the signs of Neolithic to Bronze Age occupation. These newer settlers were agriculturalists and they brought a religious culture which included burying their dead in megalithic tombs. There are many tomb remains and there must have been many more that have

Parc y Meirw ('field of the dead') is on a slope of the Gwaun valley. An alignment of stones is 138 ft (42 m) long with four pillars still standing.

since been destroyed. Pentre Ifan, easily reached south of Newport, is an astonishing example of one of these 'cromlechs', surely the finest in Britain. There is another example near Longhouse, 'Carreg Samson'.

The period around 3000 BC saw the mysterious erection of standing stones and stone circles, sometimes within ditched enclosures – the henges. Gors Fawr on the south side of Preseli is hardly a spectacular circle but is enigmatic. It consists of a remaining sixteen stones in a diameter of around 70 ft (21 m). Two stones to the north-east must have had some relevance. There are many standing stones in the park and their significance is long lost. Sometimes stones are placed in an alignment.

The placing of the stones, and the places where they came from, must have had great significance. For here in the Preseli Hills, on Carnmeini (or Carnmenyn as it appears on maps), originated one of Britain's greatest mysteries. The highly organised builders of Stonehenge, 135 miles (217 km) away as the crow flies, came here to dig out and collect slabs of dolerite, the 'blue stones'. There were probably around eighty of them weighing up to four tons each, which they then transported to Stonehenge,

together with the sandstone altar stone from Cosheston near Pembroke. 'How' is a matter for theories. 'Why' is unanswerable.

The 'hill forts' are thought to have their origins in the settlement of the Iron Age Celts. All that remains of them now are ditches, mounds and stones, sometimes the signs of hut circles. They were probably built with wooden stockades. Some of the most spectacular sites are on the headlands, for instance on the tip of St David's Head. There are traces on the top of the Marloes Peninsula, and on Gateholm Island. Inland the remains worth seeing are at Garn Fawr at the southern end of Strumble Head, Foel Drygarn on the south-eastern side of the Preseli Hills, and at Mynydd Carningli south of Newport.

There is no sign in the park of Roman military

St Govan's Chapel, near Bosherston, stands on the site of a Celtic hermitage.

presence. This south-west corner of Wales was effectively contained by a road running north east from Carmarthen (*Maridunum*) and the inhabitants here were probably peaceful. However, tribal rivalries may have resulted in the continuing use of the hill forts up to the Dark Ages. The late Roman to Dark Age period also saw a number of Irish incursions into Pembrokeshire; the area has continued to have close links with Ireland to this day. But the fifth and sixth centuries saw the spread of Christianity. Although there is no sign today of

Celtic monasteries there are other Celtic religious remains: St Govan's Chapel (recently restored by the Park Authority) and a burial ground at St Bride's Haven. There is an astonishingly well preserved Celtic cross at Carew with ingenious geometrical designs. This is one of the best in Britain. It is matched by another well preserved one at Nevern. Another, with quite different decorations of plant and animal motifs, is in the church at Penally near Tenby.

Tŷddewi (St David's house) was one of the early monasteries which had to survive the Viking raids. In fact, it has been a cathedral since Celtic times and when the Normans came in the eleventh century it was prospering and the newcomers 'adopted' it, rebuilding the cathedral.

The Normans imposed their will here as elsewhere, first from simple 'motte and bailey' strongpoints, and later with substantial stone castles. We can see castle remains today around the park. Some were centres holding a line known as the 'Landsker' separating the 'English' speaking in the south of Pembrokeshire from the Welsh speaking north of the line.

When the Norman Roman church system ousted

Carreg Samson at Longhouse near Abercastle was a 'passage grave' once covered by a circular mound.

the Celtic, the priesthood at St David's was replaced by a powerful and wealthy Norman bishopric. The Norman church edifice which replaced the old building is sitting in its sheltered hollow on the otherwise wind-swept peninsula. It looks austere, but see it when the sun comes out after a rain storm and the beauty of the still-wet stone glows, for amongst the grey sandstone are stones of a delicate purple colour – like crushed blackberry.

was once a staple industry. Some of the quarries provided high-grade roofing slates which were shipped, and later railed, to many parts of Britain. Spectacular slate quarry remains are visible at Rosebush with others at Porthgain harbour and Abereiddi. The limestone in south Pembrokeshire was also used extensively, with kilns on almost every creek and haven. As well as agricultural fertiliser, it was used for mortar and rendering on buildings, thus influencing the style of architecture in the area. The railways eventually promoted the holiday trade. Tenby became very popular and continues so, happily spared the worst of blatant commercial vulgarity.

Despite the decline of the oil industry and the recent closure of one refinery and a larger terminal,

Saundersfoot was once a busy port shipping the coal from local mines. Now it is a pleasant holiday resort.

The interior is a revelation. The present cathedral was begun in the twelfth century by Bishop Peter de Leia and what is seen in the nave is largely of this period; in 1220 de Leia's tower collapsed on what would have been beyond. It was rebuilt and then all improved in the fourteenth century under Bishop Henry Gower, who also built the Lady Chapel. Gower's masterpiece was the beautiful rood screen. He also enlarged and improved the nearby Bishop's Palace. In the fifteenth and sixteenth centuries the Norman roof was replaced by the wonderful oak ceiling and the tower height raised. The cathedral survived the Dissolution but the palace was abandoned soon after and is now a superb ruin.

The way of life here has been as enduring as the cathedral. There was agriculture in the south, where cattle and sheep were kept; there was fishing from the small ports with some trade to the larger ones and there was some mining. Coal measures between west Carmarthen Bay and St Bride's Bay were exploited from the sixteenth century. The industry peaked in the nineteenth and then died in the early twentieth century. The signs of the industry which once affected the Daugleddau area and St Bride's Bay have largely gone. Quarrying

St David's Cathedral. Two pilgrimages to St David's were once regarded as equal to one to Rome. The Conqueror himself was here. Henry II came hoping to be absolved of guilt for the murder of Becket, and Edward I came with his queen.

the present main industry is still the oil refining centred on Milford Haven where large tankers can make good use of the deep-water facilities. Compared with the beauty of its surroundings, the complex is a disaster area. But full marks to the companies for trying hard to minimise the visual effect with colouring and landscaping, and for striving to maintain a clean operation. There is liaison with the Park Authority and methods of dealing with oil spills, thankfully infrequent, have been pioneered.

Taking into account the whole area of the park, the impact of the refineries is not great. The same can be said of the military presence in Pembrokeshire. Although the military ranges are not always open to public access, they are managed in agreement with the Park Authority and other conservation interests. Splendid wildlife areas are the result and the National Park organises frequent guided walks through restricted areas.

The military zone west of Elegug Stacks to Freshwater West is the only length of coastline not open to the walker, who can otherwise enjoy the coastal path which has been negotiated, created and maintained by the Park Authority. I saw the beginnings of the operation and when it was explained I could hardly believe that it could be done. It is there – 186 miles (299 km) of it – and a magnificent achievement. John Barrett, who had much to do with its development, wrote the first official guide in 1974. Of course, it has many access points from the highways and the visitor need not be a long-distance walker to enjoy it. Much of the park

can be seen using a combination of vehicle transport and foot.

Only some selected places can be referred to here. Dinbych-y-Pysgod – 'the little fort of the fish', or Tenby – is a good touring centre and a superb little town with its intact medieval walls and remains of its castle. To the south of Amroth (several bays away from Tenby) where the coast path begins is

Manorbier Castle. In the twelfth century Gerald, archdeacon of Brecon, called this place 'the pleasantest spot in Wales'.

Wiseman's Bridge where in 1943 Winston Churchill watched a dress rehearsal for the D-Day landings. A National Park Information Centre at Kilgetty gives an account of the area's former coal mining industry.

Off-shore south of Tenby is lovely Caldey Island to which one can take a boat. The curiosity here is the little thirteenth–fourteenth century chapel with a crooked spire. There was once a Celtic monastery here, sacked by the Vikings, and a variety of monastic establishments on the island over the centuries. The present one is Cistercian. The monks farm the island and sell their produce, which includes a wide range of perfumes and toiletries.

Moving on along the coastal strip there is Manorbier village with its picturesque castle. Some miles to the west beyond Freshwater East's fine beach, Bosherston Lily Ponds National Nature Reserve extends from Stackpole Head to the splendid sands of Broad Haven South. To the west again is a most spectacular sight: Elegug Stacks, great pillars of rock alive with birds in spring and early summer. Nearby is the great natural arch: 'The Green Bridge of Wales'.

Inland an exploration of the valley of the

Strumble Head from Garn Fawr. The Park organises open days at the lighthouse, in agreement with Trinity House, the National Lighthouse Association.

Carew Castle, leased by the Park Authority.

Round the promontory of Wooltack Point at Martins Haven boat trips take nature enthusiasts to the National Nature Reserve on Skomer Island, and also to the bird observatory on Skokholm Island. Both places blaze with wild flowers and are loud with sea birds.

Broad Haven is to the north with extensive

Skomer Island Nature Reserve. A rabbit-proof enclosure reveals what plants will thrive without grazing.

Daugleddau, where the Park Authority has made new footpaths, is recommended. Carew is at its south-eastern end. The castle (dating from the twelfth century) is an unforgettable picture. A thousand year-old Celtic cross is near the castle entrance. Upton Castle is to the west of Carew and not open to the public, but thanks to a management agreement with the Park Authority the grounds are open, and they have a fine collection of trees and shrubs.

Just outside the park the old town of Haverfordwest with medieval castle and churches is worth a visit. It is a friendly place (I admit to a bias since my mother spent her childhood years here) and it is a good touring centre.

Westwards along the coast there is the pleasant little village of Dale on the way to St Ann's Head, an outstanding viewpoint, and the Marloes promontory with a good stretch of beach.

At Gateholm Island there are traces of rectangular huts, probably dating from the Dark Ages. Although Gateholm can be reached at low tide, it is not easy to scramble on to it. The tides on this coast can be very high so visitors are advised to check their times and also to be careful on the cliffs.

beaches and impressive cliffs. One of the Park's eight visitor centres is located here, a good source of information about activities, including boat trips, walks and talks. Northwards again there are two miles of sands at Newgale and the road and path westwards for St David's pass through the pretty harbour village of Solva.

St David's, the country's smallest city, has a number of attractions, in addition to the cathedral and palace which have been mentioned already, including a demonstration farm, small museums and art galleries. The wind-swept peninsula, though, has many traces of old settlements and an Iron Age fort is on the Head. From St Justinian's there is a boat service to Ramsay Island where there is a breeding colony of grey seals and of course more flowers and birds. North-eastwards the coastline continues magnificently, past Abereiddi and its Blue Lagoon

and picturesque Porthgain, to Strumble Head by another grey seal area. The Head is another great viewpoint. Not far away is Carregwastad Point, site of the last invasion of Britain, by the French in 1797. Beyond is Dinas Head and Needle Rock.

Newport, an ancient borough with a Norman church and remains of a castle, has a good museum and a park information centre. At Nevern, to the north east, the castle remains are owned by the local community council (with a little help from the Park Authority). The splendid Celtic cross is in the churchyard. Beyond, the coastal path continues wildly to the great viewpoint climax at Cemaes Head, descending to the broad sweep of Poppit Sands and the northern boundary of the path beside the Teifi estuary.

A retreat to Fishguard, with its attractive Lower Town, gives access to the beautiful Gwaun valley. Some of it is protected by Sites of Special Scientific Interest and as park-leased property. The Gwaun is fed from the moors of Mynydd Preseli, the Preseli Hills. One of the hills' popular viewpoints on Foel Eryr (Eagle's Peak) is easily reached from the B4329 road, but the highest point is east of this at Foel Cwmcerwyn. An ancient track runs east to west along the crest-line and the hills about are full of ancient sites; the stone circle in the south east, the defensive settlement and hut circles on Foel Drygarn to the north east, and Pentre Ifan, that superb cromlech, is north of the B4329 north of Brynberian.

But it is towards the eastern end of the Preseli summits that the 'blue stones' outcrop among the wind-blown grass and heather. And the question remains to haunt: why did the builders of far, far away Stonehenge come here for their stone? It could only be that this site was sacred. There is that strange feeling of 'place' that singles one out above all others. The feeling for the sea which is in all of us draws us for recreation to the rim of the land. The sea, and also the cliffs and beaches, the moors and rivers, the birds and flowers are the components of the Pembrokeshire Coast's dramatic pageantry, but the total effect is greater than the sum of its parts. Whoever comes here is compelled to return.

The small harbour of Abercastle.

Snowdonia National Park

Anyone approaching Snowdonia for the first time can hardly fail to be astonished at the gradual change in the scenery as the road winds by woods and watercourses, and as rugged mountains appear nearer and higher, heap upon heap, shoulder to shoulder. This feels a different country. Even the road signs display an unfamiliar language.

Snowdonia is superbly beautiful country with nine mountain ranges, each with a remarkably distinct character of its own. In between them, and coastwards, is a delightfully varied landscape of surprises: passes, woodlands and forest, green valleys, lakes and rivers, small settlements, coastal plains and sandy beaches.

It is not easy to describe the effect that the

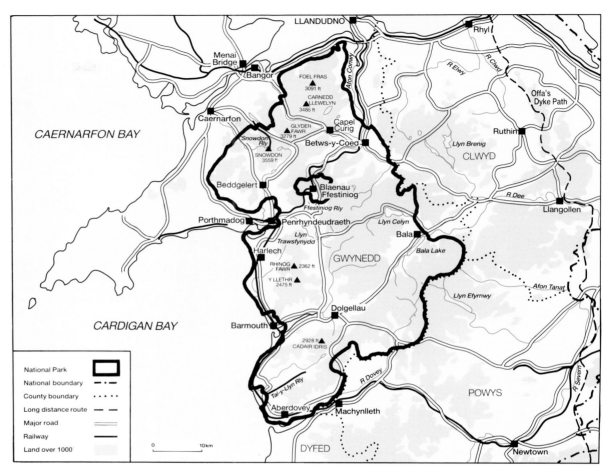

Year of designation	1951
Area	838 sq miles (2,171 sq km)
Population	23,761 (1981)
Land use (approx)	
Enclosed farmland	21%
Open country	60%
Commercial forestry	12%
Deciduous woodland	2%
Land ownership (approx)	
National Park	0.5%
Forestry Commission	15.6%
Water Authority	6%
National Trust	8.7%
Natural areas of special interest	
National Nature Reserves	17
Forest Nature Reserves	12
(plus numerous other nature reserves)	
Sites of Special Scientific Interest	45
Historical sites	
Archaeological	137 listed
	(possibly 5% of whole)
In guardianship	15

Administering authority
Snowdonia National Park Committee,
Snowdonia National Park Offices,
Penrhyndeudraeth,
Gwynedd
LL48 6LS
Tel: (0766) 770274
The national park is wholly within the county of Gwynedd

Left:
Snowdonia National Park – a formidable and beautiful intimacy of mountains.

mountains can have on the senses. Comparisons are made with the mountains of the Lake District. But there the English peaks show a maturity, an ordered settled sternness, and there is a feeling of permanence. By comparison some of the mountains of Snowdonia can give the impression that they were thrust out of the molten earth-core in the chaos of yesterday; and today and tomorrow – who knows? The Ice Age carved the Lake District. It savaged the much greater heights of Snowdonia. There are three peaks above 3,000 ft (914 m) in the Lake District; there are fourteen in Snowdonia and around fifteen between 2,000 and 3,000 ft.

Even so, by alpine standards the heights are not

Snowdonia National Park.

Any exploration of Snowdonia is better appreciated if some of the common place name elements (such as 'llyn' for lake, 'coed' for wood) are known. A glossary can be obtained from the park's information service.

So to the main attraction. The Snowdon range is a very distinct, compact mass covering some 16 sq miles (41 sq km). Yr Wyddfa is the glorious shapely summit and the highest point in England and Wales, 3,559 ft (1,085 m). Spreading from it are five high arms; long ones to the north and north-west, sharp ridges with deep hollows to the east, south-east and south-west. These too have their peaks, not much lower than Yr Wyddfa. The most remote, Yr Aran, 2,451 ft (747 m), has splendid prospects to the north-west and south-east, and an uninterrupted view up along the ridge to Yr Wyddfa. The south-eastern arm is Y Lliwedd, 2,947 ft (893 m), with its astonishing precipices piled above the long lake of Llyn Llydaw. Here Welsh rock climbing was born in the late nineteenth century. The eastern arm, the enormous bulk of Crib Goch, 3,023 ft (921 m), on the north side of Llyn Llydaw offers the really exciting ridge walk. The view from the crown is stupendous. But the mountaineer's eye will turn with anticipation

Snowdon from the south-east across Cwm Llan.

great. But impressiveness has little to do with height. The visual effect is a matter of proportions and the close relationships of forms. The enormity of an alpine peak can only be appreciated at a distance. At its footings there is merely a general awareness of the great magnitude; the summit is remote. But by Snowdon and among the Glyders – among the poised and soaring ramparts, columns, pinnacles, folds, warps and knolls, buttresses and recesses – there is a formidable intimacy. At once it locks onto imagination. It compels reaction.

The mountains here have been the training ground of some of the world's greatest mountaineers; and no mountaineer, no matter how well travelled, can fail to be excited by the peaks and crags of Snowdonia.

The region has been a natural fortress with the mountains forming a barrier to the east, and the sea to the west. Hence its particular character has been defended, helping the inhabitants to preserve their own special culture: the traditions of community welfare, art, religion, hospitality. This is the ancient kingdom of Gwynedd, the true heart of Wales with the old poetic 'Cymraeg', the Welsh language. Language unifies, gives identity.

'A formidable and beautiful intimacy of mountains.' Snowdonia range. The summit, Yr Wyddfa, is in the background with Crib Goch left foreground.

Llanberis, 'Pen-y-pass'. The 'Miners' Track' climbs to Llyn Llydaw, crosses the foot of the lake by a causeway and goes by the second lake of Glaslyn to the summit ridge. But the 'Pyg Track' is surely one of the most used mountain paths in Britain. This takes a higher line with great views over the surprisingly blue waters of Llyn Llydaw and Glaslyn.

So to the summit of all, Yr Wyddfa. What can one say? The panorama from the summit cairn, if luck is with you and there is no mist, is superb; but the immediate surroundings rather less so. Legend has it that here is the grave of the giant Rhita Fawr. If so part of it could now be below the concrete of what might look like a missile silo, but is in fact a café. Any man-made structure would be out of place on a mountain summit. The best that can be said for this is that it is *infinitely* better than the former mess it replaced, and the National Park Authority has spent a great deal of money improving the facilities on Snowdon. The high and remote feeling that one might expect from a summit is rare during the holiday season. One is likely to be shoulder to shoulder with all the colourful varieties of humanity, not all mountaineers, for this is the terminus of the famous mountain railway. No such enterprise would

The 'Pyg Track' route to the summit.

to the ridge leading inwards to Yr Wyddfa and guarded by rock pinnacles, which at close quarters offer little difficulty; but this scramble should be regarded as for the experienced only, and in good weather. The route leads over the range's second highest peak, Crib y Ddysgl, 3,495 ft (1,065 m), with arguably the farthest views of all.

The northern arm curves round to Llanberis and offers an easy popular route to and from the summit, with a view westwards to the other perpendicular cliffs above a little lake under the north-western arm. This precipice is Clogwyn Du'r Arddu; affectionately 'Cloggy' to climbers, long one of the most important rock-climbing areas in Britain. Along the ridge of Clogwyn Du'r Arddu comes the popular 'Snowdon Ranger' route from the west. One other route from the west is the Rhyd Ddu whose top section at Bwlch Main can be hazardous in a gale! The great route from the south is the 'Watkin Path'. This follows an old miners' route from Nantgwynant, then a steeper zig zag path; a way engineered for Sir Edward Watkin, a nineteenth century tycoon who had a chalet in the valley.

The most popular routes start, naturally, from the highest road side point, at the top of the Pass of

Cwm Llan. Start of the 'Watkin Path'.

get planning permission in a national park nowadays, but the rack railway has been there since 1896 after only a year in the building. Its route winds up 3,140 ft (957 m) from Llanberis in a little less than 5 miles (8 km), on an 800 mm gauge. The views from the hour-long ride are good, particularly down the cwms to Llanberis Pass, and westwards into Clogwyn Du'r Arddu. This could be the nearest thing to flying without actually leaving the ground. The diesel locomotives, well engineered though they may be, are a smelly intrusion. It is the superb, sturdy little steam engines of racing revs and crawling cog that are appealing. The sound is a distinctive feature of holiday-time Snowdon: 'I-can-do-it-I-can-do-it-I-can-do-it'.

But the character of Snowdon changes completely in the winter, when the frozen massif is strictly the preserve of well-equipped and experienced mountaineers.

The superb range of the Glyders lies in a curve north-east of the Snowdon range and offers some of the best mountaineering challenges in the country with five peaks over 3,000 ft (914 m). The highest, Glyder Fawr, 3,279 ft (999 m), walls the side of the scenic Pass of Llanberis. At its foot, overhanging the

Mist swirls around the Glyder crags.

Llyn Idwal with Y Garn beyond.

pass, are the three sheer crags famed in climbing circles: from east to west Dinas y Gromlech, Garreg Wastad, and Clogwyn y Crochan. The southern view is all bulk; the view from the north is quite different, showing astonishing lines of great cliffs and 'cwms' (English 'combe', Scottish 'corrie'), text-book examples of hollows scooped out in the Ice Age. The climbs are all superb and the summit ridge is a chaos of great boulders and rocks. Tryfan, 3,010 ft (917 m) at the range's eastern end is a most distinct feature with its three-peaked ridge, looking like a great petrified dinosaur. 'Milestone buttress', a popular climbers' training crag, is at its northern end.

Ogwen, at the foot of Llyn Ogwen by the A5, is the great centre for the Glyders, and a relatively easy path takes anyone (including babes in push-chairs!) into the cwm, to the edge of the fine lake of Llyn Idwal, the centre of which is a National Nature Reserve. Beyond is the great climbers' scene. The crags about are now largely used for training, including the well-known Idwal Slabs; but at the head is the popular route, through boulders and up by the cleft of Twll Du ('black hole'), otherwise known as 'The Devil's Kitchen', to Glyder Fawr. To

Llyn Idwal, in a National Nature Reserve.

South again are the Rhinogs (Rhinogydd), a twenty-mile long ridge of the park's oldest rocks, south-east of Harlech, largely rough and heather-covered. This range is for those who like solitude, for this is the nearest the park has to wilderness. The highest peak is Y Llethr, 2,475 ft (756 m). A popular exploration is from the beautiful Llyn Cwm Bychan and up into the cwm by a paved way, the 'Roman Steps', probably not Roman but certainly ancient.

East again, and west of Bala lake are more heather-covered hills, the Arenigs. Arenig Fawr, the highest at 2,801 ft (854 m) has very extensive views. South-eastwards are the Arans, a ridge of several miles with Aran Fawddwy rising to 2,971 ft (905 m). Access here is restricted, the park's information service will advise.

The southernmost range is the dominant and majestic Cadair Idris, seen so distinctly from Dolgellau. It has a beautiful character of its own with another of those splendidly wild and haunting scenes – across the waters of Llyn Cau to the soaring crags of the cwm. The highest peak is at 2,928 ft (892 m). Because of the mountain's relative isolation it offers the park's greatest views over the sea, and over the hills and lakes to the heights of Snowdon.

the east another great, wilder cwm holds Llyn Bochlwyd with other climbers' crags under Glyder Fach, the second highest in the range, 3,262 ft (994 m).

The Carneddau is the long, and largest range north of the Glyders, falling to the sea in the north and the Conwy valley to the east. It consists of broad grassy arms sprawling from a central arch. The rock is bared only in a scattering of outcrops and cliffs. Eight summits are over 3,000 ft, including Carnedd Llewelyn, 3,485 ft (1,064 m), third highest mountain in Wales.

East of Snowdon and seen well on the eastern approach to Capel Curig from Betws-y-Coed is Moel Siabod, 2,861 ft (872 m), and south of this are the Moelwyns. The most spectacular peak is Cnicht, 'the Matterhorn of Wales', seen from the south as a striking cone, but in fact on approach it is found to be a long ridge. The views from it are sublime.

Travelling south-east to Beddgelert one is struck by a handsome craggy mountain standing above the village. This is Moel Hebog, 2,566 ft (782 m). A fine walk and scramble from the village centre leads up it, offering remarkable views south-westwards across Cardigan Bay.

Carreg y Saeth. A modest height to the south of Llyn Cwm Bychan.

The great beauty of Snowdon is not all at the higher levels. At the eastern end of Llanberis Pass is the road junction by Llyn Penygwryd, and the hotel, famed haunt of climbers since the beginning of the sport. Here the mountaineers were based for their training for that first successful ascent of Everest in 1953. Southwards is the Nantgwynant road, A498. Ideally this, one of the finest scenic routes in Britain, should be traveled from its foot at the end of the Vale of Ffestiniog at Penrhyndeudraeth. From this end the road crosses the levels of Traeth Mawr with its views across to Moel Hebog, left, and as one progresses, right to Cnicht, the 'Matterhorn of Wales'. Then the lovely wooded cliffs enclose the Pass of Aberglaslyn, aflame with colour in autumn, and finally the village of Beddgelert is reached. Ideally Aberglaslyn Pass to Beddgelert should be walked, along the river's eastern bank from Pont Aberglaslyn. Beddgelert is a delightful village (sometimes, alas, snarled with traffic); once savoured it is addictive. There is a wealth of walks about at high and low levels.

The A498 then goes by Llyn Dinas, a beautiful lake below hanging woods. A pleasant footpath walk goes by the eastern bank. Continuing further Llyn

The Artro river which flows from the beautiful Llyn Cwm Bychan.

A riverside path. One of a variety of attractive walks around Beddgelert.

Gwynant is reached under the south-eastern foot of Snowdon. There are great views across to Snowdon as the road climbs, and ahead the horizon is walled by the Glyders.

Betws-y-Coed is the showpiece village beauty spot with everything to offer the visitor as a touring centre, in good walking country with lovely woodlands, river banks, waterfalls. One can hardly see this attractive village for people at times – many coached in from the nearby seaside resorts; but the place oozes welcome and hospitality. The National Park has its main Visitor Centre here.

The A5 from Betws-y-Coed goes west to the junction with the road for Llanberis and Nantgwynant at Capel Curig, another accommodation centre for mountaineers, and here is Plas-y-Brenin, the National Centre for Mountain Activities.

One scenic route goes west and south from Betws-y-Coed through the lovely vale of the Lledr by Pont-y-pant to Dolwyddelan, with its ancient castle on the hill. Further on there are good views of Snowdon and the Moelwyns before the road plunges down out of the park into the devastation of the largely abandoned slate quarries at Blaenau Ffestiniog. Here some of the slate was mined and the caverns are now open to the public. A left turn takes one back into the park to Ffestiniog (or 'Llan Ffestiniog'), an attractive village base for scenic walks and views of waterfalls. A side road here goes by the riverside to Maentwrog, another small tourist centre. Nearby across the river is Plas Tan-y-Bwlch, the National Park's Study Centre.

From Maentwrog the A470 goes south past Llyn Trawsfynydd, with its nuclear power station, towards Dolgellau with impressive views of the Rhinogydd, right. Dolgellau is a little stone country town, very busy on Friday, cattle market day. There is very good walking hereabout, including the scenic 'Precipice Walk'; and there is access to the great Cadair Idris.

Several roads meet at Dolgellau. One goes north-east by a Roman road over moorland with the Arans on the right, to Llyn Tegid (Bala Lake). This, the largest natural lake in Wales, is in the ownership of the Park and is a prime fishing and sailing lake; but scenically it lacks the drama of near heights. Bala is a country market town with a jumble of interesting and dull architecture. Among the town's thinking sons was the Reverend Thomas Charles (1755–1814), famous preacher and founder of the

The 'Roman Steps'. An ancient way through Bwlch Tyddiad in the remote Rhinogs.

British and Foreign Bible Society. A National Park Information Centre explains the history of the area.

From Dolgellau, with its own information centre, the A487 goes east and turns south-west under the crags of Cadair Idris. A branch road, the B4405 goes by Tal-y-Llyn to Tywyn, base for the Tal-y-Llyn railway, a great tourist attraction. A road goes south to Aberdyfi, a pretty harbour village where there is a National Park Information Centre. From Tywyn a northbound road goes by the coast and a toll bridge to Barmouth, just outside the park; a popular seaside holiday resort with good sandy beaches. Northwards again the road goes on, with the Rhinogydd on the right, to reach the pretty up-down-village of Harlech, dominated by the castle.

The first clear evidence of human presence in Snowdonia dates from the Neolithic period between 4000 and 2000 BC. There are good examples of burial chambers ('cromlechs') in the park, now exposed from their original stone and earthen covering. One is at Dyffryn Ardudwy between Harlech and Barmouth in what was once a school playground. There are several in the Conwy valley, notably at Maen-y-bardd in the north-east of the park, and especially by Capel Garmon, south-east of

The Afon Mawddach from the 'Precipice Walk' near Dolgellau.

Remains of a burial chamber structure at Dyffryn Ardudwy.

SH 706387). Parts of the very scenic Sarn Helen can be found and explored. Another Roman road from the Tomen-y-Mur road ran north-eastwards to Chester. This passed by Llyn Tegid, and the site of a fort can be seen at the south-eastern end of the lake at Caer Gai.

At the time of the Roman occupation, and afterwards, the inhabitants lived in round houses with stone bases or stakes. Remains of these hut circles have been found, though many, of course, are buried under more modern settlements. One site where hut circle remains can be seen is by Bryn-y-Castell, near Afon Gamallt, north-east of Ffestiniog (SH 727429). This has been excavated by students from Plas Tan-y-Bwlch, the National Park Study Centre.

Little is known about the area in the Dark Ages when the kingdom of Gwynedd emerged. After the Romans left the Christian missionaries were the new invaders, coming from the sea and along the Roman roads. There was effective resistance to Anglo-Saxon occupation. Much is legend. Was King Arthur here? And is he waiting with his warriors in a cave at Bwlch y Saethau, below Snowdon's summit, for a new call when the Britons are in dire trouble?

An artist's impression of a stake-wall round house of the type excavated by students from Plas Tan-y-Bwlch at the site near Bryn-y-Castell. It was found that the settlement must have traded in iron.

Betws-y-Coed. It is possible to walk inside this structure (leaflet at farm). Later, from the second to the first millennium BC the dead were cremated and buried in round barrows. There are many of these on the coastal plains and inland by agricultural land, and a number of impressive standing stones which probably marked old routes and boundaries.

The war-like Celts who then occupied the area were responsible for the introduction of the Welsh language. Clan rivalries probably account for the number of hill forts of earth and stone, dating from around 500 BC and lasting through the Roman period. These earthworks can still be seen in many places, a clue to their whereabouts can be found in the Welsh place names containing 'caer', 'castell', or 'gaer'. One good example is at Pen-y-gaer in the Conwy valley.

There are few signs of Roman occupation within the park. Several Roman roads entered off the Chester to Caernarfon road of Iulius Agricola. From the fort of Canovium in the Conwy valley (near Caerhun) one road, later known as 'Sarn Helen' ran inland in a southerly direction by Capel Curig to Tomen-y-Mur, south of Ffestiniog, where a fort was built (now on private land, map reference

Youngsters sit in the burial chamber near Capel Garmon, used as a stable in more recent years.

Edward became determined to bring the Welsh to heel. Following successful campaigns he consolidated his position by building more substantial castles, sensibly close to sea supply routes. The famous castles at Conwy and Caernarfon are just outside the park, but Harlech castle surpasses any for its exciting setting. There are tremendous views from its walls. The well preserved gatehouse is a massive feature. There were further revolts against English rule, notably by Owain Glyndŵr early in the fifteenth century. He took Harlech castle in 1404 and Harlech became capital of Wales, but was retaken by the English in 1408.

The history of Wales has been a struggle for preservation of national identity, of which language is a vital part. It was ironic therefore that even though the Tudors were descendants of the princes of Gwynedd and gained the throne by Welsh help, they introduced repressive laws in and following the Act of Union in 1536. Processes of law were in English and no man was allowed to take office in Wales unless English was his language. On the other hand, Elizabeth I made a vital contribution to the survival of the language by commanding that the

The still impressive Harlech castle. For a time in the fifteenth century it was the effective seat of Welsh government.

The early Norman presence saw firstly the building of law enforcement 'motte and bailey' strongpoints: a ditch around high earth mounds surmounted by a wooden structure. There are some remains to be seen in the park. One example was found on the site of the Roman fort at Tomen-y-Mur (which has since been built on), and there is another just south of Bala.

Some of the best examples of castles built by the Welsh princes are Castell Dolbadarn at Llanberis and Castell Dolwyddelan in the lovely valley of the Lledr (SH 722523), said to be the birthplace of Llewelyn the Great. Beneath Cadair Idris on its south-eastern flank is the beautifully sited ruin of yet another, Castell-y-Bere (SH 667086), sacked in 1294 when Edward I was intent on taking Wales into English sovereignty, for the Normans did not have it their own way in Wales. Llewelyn the Great ruled Gwynedd from early in the thirteenth century. He married the daughter of King John and was on good terms with the English crown, but took advantage of the unrest at the time of the Magna Carta to acquire several of the king's castles, becoming virtually the chief prince of an independent Wales. When Llewelyn II refused to pay homage to Edward I,

A distant view of Harlech castle from the north.

Lloydia serotina. The rare 'Snowdon Lily' or 'spiderwort'.

Bible be translated into Welsh in 1588.

Increasing trade with England stimulated sheep and cattle rearing, and the extensive forests which once covered the area were much further reduced. Farming has remained a main occupation of the area ever since.

Copper was mined in the area probably from Roman times. There was a working mine on Snowdon's eastern side by Llyn Llydaw into the nineteenth century. The old Sygyn Fawr mine at Beddgelert is now preserved and open to the public. Gold has been mined in Snowdonia too, and still is on a modest scale. Gold for the royal wedding rings was obtained from Gwynfynydd and Clogau mines by Coed y Brenin forest.

However, the industry that has made its mark is slate quarrying. There are many quarries, the largest being outside the park. There is a vast quarried area by Llanberis. The great artificial cliffs are now used by a new generation of gymnastic rock climbers! But it is Blaenau Ffestiniog which presents the most amazing scene of exploitation.

Tourism became the important industry it is today when the railways were developed in the nineteenth century. With the attractions of the

A locomotive of the Tal-y-Llyn railway. The old narrow gauge slate railways here and at Blaenau Ffestiniog have been restored by enthusiasts and are now great tourist attractions.

superb landscape and Snowdonia's reputation for warm hospitality, the industry has great prospects for the future.

Snowdonia has such a wide range of habitats that it is not surprising to learn that there are more National Nature Reserves here, managed by the Nature Conservancy Council, than in any other comparable area in Britain. There are seventeen, as well as some forty-five protected Sites of Special Scientific Interest (1987). Some of the oak woodlands are of international importance because of their unusual communities of mosses and liverworts.

It is only possible to mention a few points of interest in this chapter. Detailed information can be obtained from the park's information service or the Nature Conservancy Council, Penrhos Road, Bangor. Botanically the sheep-grazed mountains with exposed acidic rock are attractive but offer little to excite. The pleasurable finds are the arctic-alpine flora which grow on north-facing sheep-proof ledges and gullies where leached minerals are available. The only real rarity is the spiderwort, or 'Snowdon lily', *Lloydia serotina*, which grows nowhere else in Britain. The birds of the crags include the raven and the peregrine falcon, which has made a comeback after declining due to the use of pesticides. The chough seems to prefer the artificial crags of abandoned quarries. The wandering goats are now the mountain animal. Once domesticated they are hardly 'wild' in the true sense but wild enough in any other sense.

Below the heights the interest is in finding communities of not-so-rare plants in odd positions where one would not expect to see them. Some of the broadleaved woodlands are rich in flora. The most interesting animal is the polecat, fairly common here but almost extinct in other areas of Britain. The other, rarer predator, the pine marten, is seldom seen. Of the migrant birds the pied flycatcher is common in Snowdonia, but very infrequent elsewhere.

The coastal dunes and estuaries do not fail the plant spotter. Here one can find the pretty seaside pansy. *Viola curtisii*, the bloody cranesbill, the marsh helleborine and the northern marsh orchid.

Of the fish, apart from the migrant salmon and trout entering the estuaries, the brown trout is very common, but only grows to a large size when the food is good. Char, a sort of deep-water trout, is found in Llyn Cwellyn, and Llyn Bodlyn by the Rhinogydd. One whitefish, related to the rare

Welsh poppy.

A hill farm in Snowdonia.

park large areas were covered by alien conifer trees. Indeed, some of the first plantings were made here when the Forestry Commission was formed in 1919. Meanwhile native broadleaved woodlands, now reduced to two and a half per cent of the area, are still under threat. The National Park Authority's woodlands officer's vital task is to help landowners preserve native woodlands, offering help with fencing and planting where necessary, and liaising with the Forestry Commission in furthering a 'broadleaved' policy. More blanket conifer forestry is opposed.

There are other problems which need dealing with continually and all cannot be listed here. Footpath erosion is one, particularly on Snowdon, the summit of which is reached on foot by an estimated quarter of a million annually. With support from the Countryside Commission the Authority launched a Snowdon management scheme in 1979. A tremendous amount of path repair and restoration work has been done since. Snowdon's 'Pyg Track' has had special attention. The maintenance of all paths is a continuing concern, shared with the National Trust staff on land in their ownership. But not all paths are rights of

Snowdon's 'Pyg Track', the most popular mountain path in Britain, extensively repaired and reinforced by the Park Authority.

whitefish of the Lake District, is the Gwyniad, found only in Llyn Tegid and nowhere else in Britain.

Snowdonia's main problems – the economic uncertainties of hill farming, the decline in rural industries and diminishing rural populations – are the same as any other highland region of Britain, but writ large. No ordinary farmer could survive in the harsh hill conditions of Snowdonia. It requires a special breed of men with the inherited experience of many generations. Their numbers have suffered an alarming decline. If the national park is to preserve its living landscape, the Authority must continue to do all it can to support hill farming.

The Park, as a planning authority, must have the protection of the environment as a priority; but every prospect for the provision of local work has to be carefully and urgently considered. The demand for slate has diminished with an accompanying loss of jobs. Some mining continues. However, a renewal of metal mining activity using modern methods of extraction, with huge, often toxic, waste deposits, needs to be opposed. The Authority has successfully discussed a compromise scheme with one mining company.

Long before Snowdonia was designated a national

way; an agreement between a landowner and the Authority has secured access on 'courtesy paths' in the Arans above Bala.

To prevent possible difficulties arising between farmers or landowners and visitors, the park's wardens, supported by volunteers, play a vital part. The wardens also make a vital contribution to mountain safety in their advisory work, and also in rescue. An additional mountain safety facility is the park's telephone weather forecast service. (Llanberis 870120).

Not only paths are eroded by public pressure; trampled sand dunes losing their cover of sea-couch and marram grass suffer 'blow-outs'. One conservation project on Harlech's shore dunes has involved the cooperation of the Park Authority, a neighbouring landowner, the local councils, and the Nature Conservancy Council.

A view from Plas Tan-y-Bwlch. Once the eighteenth century home of a prominent wealthy family, the house is now the National Park's residential study centre.

Access to the remoter areas of national parks is not always possible without private transport and walkers are restricted to circular walks within these areas. But around Snowdon the Authority has organised and subsidised a frequent bus service, the 'Sherpa', which stops and picks up at any safe point on each circuit.

Each park has a statutory duty to promote the public enjoyment of the area. The Visitor Centre at Betws-y-Coed, and five other Information Centres help to fulfil this task. But of prime importance is the Park's Residential Study Centre, at Plas Tan-y-Bwlch, offering a wide variety of countryside courses each year. There could be no better setting; it is within reach of the sea, woods, delectable green valleys, and the ramparts and crests, knuckles, folds and cwms of those magnificent mountains.

Small settlements and farms among hills and meadows. A typical rural scene in northern Snowdonia.

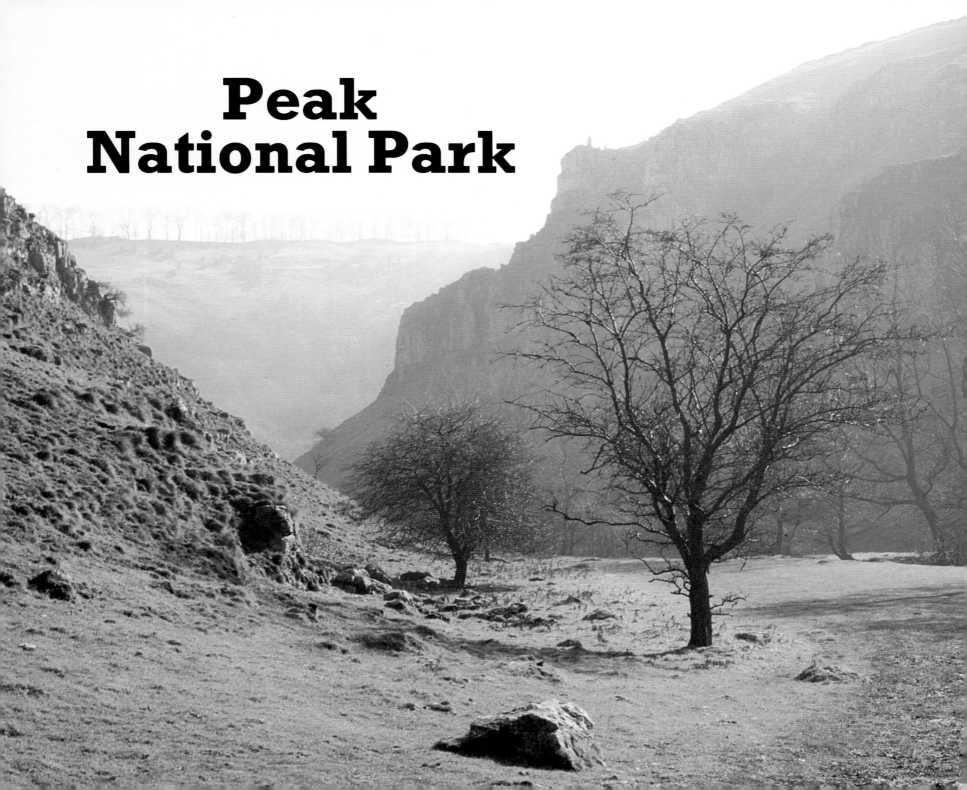

Peak
National Park

When you have enjoyed a place in the country in the happily remembered past you should be wary about a desire to return. It can bring disappointment. Landscapes change; memory cannot be trusted. So it was with some caution that my steps took me down to my old acquaintance, the River Wye under the soaring cliff of Chee Tor. I had not been there for years. It had not changed at all; the river was still as clear and the cliffs as awesome as when I first saw them as a lad. I was tempted on by the river and along the Monsal Trail down into Millers' Dale, through that amazing gorge landscape of limestone crags and giant towers. It still delighted. On then to experience that sort of fearful joy of anticipation when a forgotten happy memory filters, then floods suddenly and warmly, back into consciousness. I was among the trees at

Year of designation	1951
Area	542 sq miles (1,404 sq km)
Population	37,368 (1981)
Land use (approx)	
Enclosed farmland	49%
Open country	39%
Commercial forestry	4.5%
Deciduous woodland	2.5%
Land ownership (approx)	
National Park	4.2%
Forestry Commission	.5%
Water Authorities	13.0%
National Trust	9.7%
Natural areas of special interest	
National Nature Reserves	1
Sites of Special Scientific Interest	55

Administering authority
The Peak Park Joint Planning Board,
Aldern House,
Baslow Road,
Bakewell,
Derbyshire,
DE4 1AE
Tel: (062981) 4321
The national park is mainly in Derbyshire, with parts in Staffordshire, Cheshire, Greater Manchester, South Yorkshire and West Yorkshire.

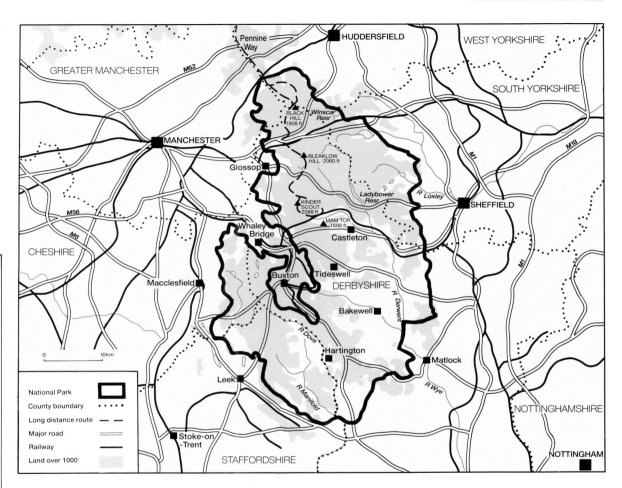

Left:
Peak National Park; contrasting landscapes of 'dark' and 'white'.

Cressbrook and I knew what view I would see as I went on and turned the corner to Monsal Head.

A return to the Peak District is like returning to a friend. It never disappoints after many years. It was a bus or a cycle ride away from the town where I was raised. My first Boy Scout camps were here, where I learned the craft of map reading and hill walking. Here I did my first back-packing expeditions ('hike-camping' in those days). I passed my First Class hike test here and did my first rock climb on Laddow. Castleton with its caverns, cliffs and castle was Shangri-la. The vast high peat plateau of Bleaklow was the Gobi Desert in summer;

Peak National Park.

There are really two Peak Districts and both are exciting: the Dark Peak and the White Peak. But it is necessary to understand first that 'peak' here does not mean the accepted idea of a sharp mountain top. 'Peak' in this area's sense comes from Old English *Peāc*, a mound or hill. (In the Anglo-Saxon Chronicle it was *Peāclond*.) 'Low' occurs here frequently too, as in Bleaklow, but it does not mean low in the accepted physical sense. Here it could mean high. It comes from the Old English *Llāw*, an old burial mound, usually to be found on high land.

The Dark Peak surrounds the national park on the west, north and east like a mantle. Its title comes from its base rock, the darker-coloured millstone grit; and inside its boundary there is an area of shale. This separates it from the White Peak with its light-coloured limestone, which covers the park's centre southwards.

Put simply, the history of the visible landscape is as follows. Between 325 and 360 million years ago the area was covered in a warm sea rich in animal life. Masses of debris formed on the sea bed

Winnats Pass, Castleton. Some say that this is where British national parks began. Mass rallies of thousands of walkers campaigned here for national parks and access to the hills in the 1920s and 30s.

the ice fields of the South Pole in winter. Kinder Scout was our Everest. Later a motorcycle took me to the Peak's enclaves I had never dreamed of.

I am not alone. It is certain that the Peak District has brought more pleasure and sense of adventure to more people than any other place in Britain, and probably in Europe! Particularly so since it became a national park and access was opened to once prohibited places. For it is surrounded by the industrial heartland of England, and around a third of the country's population live within fifty miles of its boundaries.

Because of this it was exactly right that the Peak National Park was the first park to be designated. It lost no time in pioneering the essentials, including access agreements to the hills, and the formation of Ranger and Information Services.

The River Wye in Chee Dale.

including shells, bony structures of animals and stalked sea-creatures or 'crinoids'. The beds formed limestone with a thickness of 2,450 ft (750 m). During this time there was also volcanic activity in some areas, with lava flows.

There then followed a period when the whole

The limestone gorge, Wolfscote Dale.

Harder limestones stand proud over the deepened valleys. Chrome Hill in Upper Dovedale, though of modest height, looks like a true mountain.

became part of a great river delta, and sand, mud and grit covered the limestone. This formed what are now the millstone grits and shales. Occasionally the water level dropped, allowing rich plant growth in the swamps, but in time these were inundated and died to produce coal seams, which occur more thickly east and west of the park boundary.

At the end of this Carboniferous period around 280 million years ago the land was subjected to the lifting action of great earth movements. This tilted the area upwards, high in the north and dipping to the south, east and west. The higher areas were eroded by subsequent storms, and upper layers of coal, shale and millstone grit were swept away from a large area, exposing the lower limestone. Further surface deposition occurred during the Permian and Triassic periods. Then eventually came the Ice

Ages. The slow-moving glaciers stripped off the later layers of rock and left boulder clay behind on the lee of hills. Melt water with later storm and frost periods were the last shaping force; carving out the river courses and cutting deep down into the softer rocks to make the gorges, some of them now dry and characteristic of the White Peak. Some of the harder rocks which resisted the erosive flow formed peaks, or were left standing as isolated towers. High gritstone ridges were stripped of cover and eroded to form 'tors' and the typical broken 'edges'. Water worked its way down through the limestone to form caverns and underground rivers. Unstable shale masses crumbled into land slides. The process, of course, continues to this day.

The land forms, then, are extremely varied. In

good climatic conditions after the last ice advance, the earth gradually became green and flowered. The forests began their advance. Limestone caves were used by the hunters of Paleolithic (Old Stone Age) times. They were most probably nomads following the animal herds. Tools, knives and hunting weapons, plus the bones of prey, dating to before 6000 BC have been found in caves and rock shelters in Upper Lathkill Dale, south west of Bakewell, and in the Manifold and Dove valleys in the south of the park.

During the Middle Stone Age the land was covered in forest to the higher land of the Dark Peak, and we know that hunters were active there too, for their flint spear and arrow heads and barbs have been found in wide areas. By around 3000 BC agriculture began to develop as the main means of livelihood, particularly among the better lands of the White Peak. Remains of the farmers' chambered

Arbor Low henge. A high bank 250 ft in diameter surrounds a 30 ft wide ditch. Inside it is a stone circle of 47 stones, 150 ft in diameter, with three stones in a central cove. All the huge stones are, however, lying flat; there is no real clue why. The circle was obviously of great significance, for the labour involved in the making would be considerable. The structure has two entrances, north and south.

Alport Castles. Land slips of unstable shales and grits continue. Mam Tor, near Castleton, 'The Shivering Mountain', still crumbles. The instability forms the weird shapes of Alport Castles, Alport Dale, north of the A57.

tombs have been found in a number of areas. The best known is on Minninglow east of the High Peak Trail, near the south-eastern park boundary. It had four chambers, but the covering cairn has wasted. There is also one on high land by Five Wells, west of Taddington, which had two chambers.

It was in the later Neolithic period that the henges and stone circles began to be built. The most notable in the park is Arbor Low henge, east of Parsley Hay on the A515. It is a very atmospheric,

strangely moving place. The henge must have been a tribal focal point for centuries later. From 2000 BC people of the Bronze Age lived in these high places, and presumably in the lower places occupied to the present day. Bronze Age burials often occupy the areas similarly used by earlier inhabitants. There is a burial cairn beside Arbor Low henge; and hundreds of such cairns scattered all over the park, many of them identified by the word 'low'. They were once treated with superstition. However, since

Victorian times robberies of the graves have been very extensive.

One of the most remarkable areas for Bronze Age remains in the north of England is on Stanton Moor, in the south east of the park. In a tight area over seventy burial mounds have been found. The Nine Ladies stone circle is also here and mysteriously (as

The Nine Ladies stone circle on Stanton Moor.

at other similar sites in Britain) a single stone – here the 'King's Stone' – stands just outside it. North east of Baslow at the southern end of Big Moor is Swine Sty settlement which was shown to us by a park ranger some years ago. Here, again in a small area, are earthworks, signs of field patterns, stone rings, stone circles and field clearance cairns. Investigations since have dated the activity to between 1800 and 1400 BC and surmised that the people were pastoralists; but as they ground grain

they may have had some arable land too. There was also a cottage industry: the making of jewellery out of shale. The site was acquired by the National Park Authority in 1984 and research continues.

The main still-visible signs of the Iron Age (into the first millenium BC) are the hundreds of hill forts scattered throughout the high land in every county of England and Wales. As can be expected there are more than a few in the Peak. They consist of an enclosure surrounded by one or more defensive ditches and banks, on a hill top commanding a good view. The most prominent and obvious in the Peak Park is its largest, on Mam Tor (the 'Shivering Mountain'), the high rounded hill of 1,695 ft (517 m) that commands a western approach to Castleton. Covering sixteen acres, the fort accommodated a village of round huts. Research shows that the site was occupied from the late Bronze Age. It is thought

Peak District customs, their meanings lost in time, are good excuses for festivity. On Oak Apple Day (29th May) in Castleton a 'king' covered in flowers rides round the town accompanied by his lady.

that many hill forts continued to be used into post-Roman times.

It has been assumed that at the Roman occupation the Peak District was sparsely populated. However, the area was important to the Romans for its wealth of lead. Ingots found around Matlock dating from the Roman period are marked with the word *Lutudarum*. Where this place was is a subject for conjecture. Buxton, *Aquae Arnemetiae*, was certainly used by the Romans as a spa long before the Victorians thought of it. A straight road ran to Buxton from Littlechester (*Derventio*); and another road can be traced running north-eastwards from it to *Navio*, a fort at Brough just south east of Hope. A road ran then in a roughly similar direction to a fort at Templeborough near Rotherham in Yorkshire. A section is identifiable east of Stanage Edge, but it eventually vanishes into the suburbs of Sheffield. Another road ran from *Navio* northwards to Woodlands Valley, then north-westwards to Manchester via *Ardotalia* west of Glossop. Here I am in my home territory for our Scout camp was on the Roman road at Doctor's Gate, and we travelled that

road, pulling our camp gear and food along from Glossop and Old Glossop on the troop's trek-cart, dismantling and manhandling when necessary. The Romans must have managed it better, but perhaps with less enthusiasm!

It should not be assumed that Roman occupation was always opposed. A civilian village grew around *Navio* and there was obviously trade to be done. The troops, too, needed grain, which could be grown in the accommodating soils of the White Peak. Up to forty farming settlements dating from

Magpie Lead Mine near Sheldon; the best preserved remains of the old industry. It was the presence of lead in the area that attracted the Romans.

Roman times have now been identified in the area. One farm, Roystone Grange, west of the High Peak Trail at the southern end of the park, has had remarkable continuity of use from the second century, through medieval times and right to the present day. The central area of the farm was acquired by the National Park Authority in 1987 for further research and interpretation.

Probably no great changes would have occurred immediately after the Romans left. What happened is guesswork. Carl Wark Fort stands upon a viewpoint on Hathersage Moor surrounded by a great rock wall. It is thought that this dates from the Dark Ages. Was it the base of a Celtic clan chief? An excavation of an Anglo-Saxon burial at Benty Grange above the Roman Buxton–to–Ashbourne road revealed, amongst other artifacts, a splendid iron war helmet dating from the seventh century. Some significant objects of the time mark the spread of Christianity. As in other upland areas there are stone crosses and cross fragments. Some thirty survive. One worn, though fine, example of the eighth century, with vigorous carving, stands in Bakewell churchyard.

The Normans did not rate the area highly. Domesday Book recorded that much of it was 'waste, woodland, unpastured, fit for hunting'. So an area of the Dark Peak and some of the high area of

Peveril Castle. This was first the seat of William Peverel, an illegitimate son of the Conqueror, and from it the forest law was enforced. When the second Peverel fell from grace the castle was adopted by Henry II who built the tower in 1175–6.

The huge gape of Peak Cavern dwarfs Castleton's cottages below it.

the White, in all about forty square miles, became a Royal Forest, subject to the strict forest laws. It remained so until the seventeenth century. Peveril Castle at Castleton is the only Norman castle ruin in the district and was the inspiration of Sir Walter Scott's novel *Peveril of the Peak*. Its position on the limestone crag is dramatic. It seems to have grown from the lush greenery which surrounds it, and to me in my formative years it was history come to life. Henry II liked the place. In 1157 he had Malcolm of Scotland here to sign over the counties of Cumberland and Northumberland to English rule. The town of Castleton below the castle was laid out to a medieval grid-iron plan which can still be seen today.

Castleton is magic. What adds to its fascination is its great caverns. The wide gape of Peak Cavern is astonishing. But there are also the Treak Cliff, the Blue John, and my own boyhood favourite, the Speedwell, reached by boat along a miners' level. The Blue John is famous for its unique blue and purple-tinted fluorspar rock. Castleton is so riddled with holes and caverns it suggests to the imagination the complicated hollow structure of coral. But everywhere supports plant growth, even when the soil is thin. The rock itself seems to sprout life.

Bakewell was a base of mine when my brother lived there. The friendly town existed at the time of the Norman occupation (*Badequella* in Domesday)

All Saints parish church, Bakewell. It probably stands on the site of a Saxon church or monastery. An eighth century cross is in the churchyard.

and must have had a Saxon church. It was granted a charter in 1254. Tideswell existed then too and got its market in 1251. The pride of Tideswell is its special church, styled 'The Cathedral of the Peak'.

Hardy cattle were pastured on the high land of the Dark Peak, and sheep flocks provided wool, then a valuable and essential product. Dairy cattle and sheep are still the farmers' mainstays in the Peak. But early there was that other source of wealth, the lead which had attracted the Romans' attention.

Lead was available in quantity. During the volcanic activity when the limestone was formed, gases and vapours condensed in fractures and cavities and crystalised as 'galena', or lead ore. There are mine workings in numerous places in the White Peak, most of them now hardly visible as they were old surface workings. But there are virtually hundreds of open shafts in the hills. There are also signs of 'bole hills', where early miners smelted the ore in crude hearths open to windward to obtain a draught.

Spring sandwort is one of the few plants which can grow on lead mine spoil heaps, The lovely flower is rare elsewhere.

The beautiful stately home of Chatsworth, owned by the Dukes of Devonshire, and enjoyed by thousands of visitors annually, was partly built from copper revenue. The mine was in the Manifold valley at Ecton Hill.

Unused millstones lie below Stanage Edge in the Derwent valley, The market for them was lost to synthetic carborundum stones.

Medieval landlords did well from their lead and wool resources. On the strength of this, the Vernon family built the wonderfully preserved medieval Haddon Hall, south of Bakewell. But lead mining really reached its peak of prosperity in the eighteenth century and continued in some places into the nineteenth. Copper, too, was mined very profitably.

Water, which was often an expensive embarrassment when it flowed into mine workings, was the great attraction to the enterprising industrialists of the latter part of the eighteenth century. Water power had long been used for corn mills and for ore crushing. It was then to be used for cotton mills. One of the finest mills was Richard Arkwright's at Bakewell. (There is a good display about it in Bakewell's Old House Museum.) The mill, in the lush little valley of Cressbrook (no misnomer, watercress and mint still grow in the shallows) by the Wye west of Great Longstone, once distilled peppermint and other aromatic herbs. But Arkwright did away with that nonsense when he built his new cotton mill on the site in 1783. Two years later it burnt down and was rebuilt. The present solid Georgian structure dates from 1815. It was common at the height of the cotton mill boom all

There are around 30,000 miles (48,000 km) of drystone walls in the park. Some of them obviously mark the boundaries of ancient field strips. Decline in farm labour means many are threatened by lack of maintenance, a matter for the Authority's concern.

over the north of England to use child labour, sometimes transported to the site from city workhouses as far away as London. The row of cottages behind the mill once housed them. The mill should be seen because of its fine setting. Alas, if it is to be maintained it needs a new purpose.

Quarrying has also been a traditional industry, since well before the park was created. At the present time it employs about 18 per cent of the area's workforce. Unfortunately, it produces some eyesores. The large Hope Valley Cement Works has been in existence for many years. Its huge bulk and tall chimney is in the middle of a delightful area. The quarrying scars, particularly the one at Eldon Hill south west of Castleton, are unfortunate to say the least. The park has to live with this industry but the Park Authority has to consider any proposed extension of activity very carefully, to protect the landscape and to respect the policies laid down in its approved structure plan. Fluorspar used in the steel and chemical industries is also extracted in some areas, leaving the problem of ugly tailing dams. One mining concern has commendably agreed a policy of backfilling the waste underground.

In common with the situation in other hill areas the farming industry has suffered a decline. It now accounts for only 10 per cent of the workforce, as small farms are taken over into viable units and work becomes mechanised. This brings social as well as economic problems. The decline adds to the unemployment total. In order to encourage employment in the park, the Park Authority has co-operated with the Rural Development Commission's programmes, is helping to establish job-creating small factory developments in some of the towns, and is working with local authorities and tourist boards on a tourism development programme for the area.

The growth of prosperity in the nineteenth century attracted the railway investors. Now most of that old rail mileage has gone. But the good news is that the Park Authority seized the initiative and opened the abandoned routes for walkers and cyclists. The concept is brilliant. The routes are a tremendous boon. Their firm and level surface makes easy going for those of us who are less physically able. The old Midland line route along the Wye Valley that John Ruskin despaired over is now the Monsal Trail. That arbiter of natural beauty would surely now approve. The Ashbourne-to-Buxton line of 1894 was closed in 1967, but was purchased by the Park Authority and its length is now the Tissington Trail. There is cycle hire provision. Similarly the 1830 Cromford-to-High Peak line died in 1967, and its abandoned route meets the Tissington Trail at Parsley Hay, and is now the High Peak Trail.

The freshwater crayfish, denizen of limestone rivers.

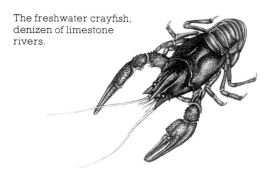

A solitary oak stands by the Snake Road in Woodlands Valley. Anciently well wooded, now only 2.5 per cent of the park is deciduous woodland. Since 1957 the Park Authority has been active in conserving and promoting woodlands. It has acquired some 600 acres of woodland in over a hundred small blocks, and has negotiated planting and management agreements with other landowners.

The old lines with their cuttings, and the river banks with their cliffs through the limestone, are perfect for the exploring botanist and entomologist, as well as for those who only wish to see and enjoy. The lime-rich river waters support flourishing plant and animal communities. I have never seen a river more densely populated than the Wye with dippers; that delightful bird whose song is so suitably liquid and which submerges in the river currents to seek food. Wagtails, too, are everywhere. The banks, particularly those that catch the sun, are ablaze with wild flowers in season.

The dipper.

Grey wagtail.

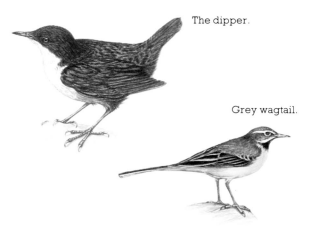

Typically the woodland growth in the White Peak is ash, sometimes with an understorey of hazel and wych elm, with willows and some alders in wet places. Ash comes into leaf late and the fall is early, allowing light and growth opportunity for the woodland ground flora.

As well as the common woodland and marsh plants there are those that flourish especially well in

lime-rich soils. There are orchids, tall mulleins in the sunny places, and cranesbills, including the showy scarlet 'bloody cranesbill'. There are rarities, too. In grazed areas those sitting on the grass might have the stemless thistle brought sharply to their attention. It normally grows only on the chalk downs of the south. Every crack and ledge in the limestone produces life: rockrose, birdsfoot trefoil, kidney vetch and stonecrop in the dry places; in the wet, liverworts, mosses and ferns, typically hart's tongue having a strong presence. The early flowering mezerion might not be uncommon in gardens but it is extremely rare in the wild. It can be found in localities here. Lathkill Dale offers such rich habitats that it is cared for as a

Mountain hare.

Red grouse.

The rare cobalt blue Jacob's ladder grows in moist areas in the limestone dales.

The cloudberry grows high on the heather moors.

National Nature Reserve. Dovedale, Monsal Dale and Cressbrook Dale are also protected.

The hay meadows alas have suffered under chemical farming methods, and grass spangled with wild flowers belongs largely to memory. But the Park Authority is trying to promote and preserve the traditionally cared-for meadows with grant aid and rural development schemes.

If the White Peak is environmentally exciting, the Dark Peak is something rather different. The vast plateaux of peat 'hags', broken by deep-channelled 'groughs', will at their best support heather, which when properly managed is home to a good grouse population. Their distinct call always evokes the Peak District to me. (I remember a Manchester fireman, called with his colleagues to help out with a runaway moorland fire, telling me that it was a dangerous job. 'Even the ducks were warning us to *go back! go back!*'). The other common bird of the

moor is the meadow pipit, but there are also curlews and golden plovers. The animal of the moor, apart from the ranging fox, is the mountain hare. It survives well, turning white in winter; which is an embarrassment when there is no snow around.

The fifty reservoirs in the park, though visually not necessarily unattractive, support little bird life. The conifer forests which surround many of them offer some support: a visiting flock of gossiping goldcrests for instance, and crossbills are also a joy to see.

There are hill-walking routes aplenty and the permutations are almost limitless. The Park's information centres and the rangers can give advice. The Pennine Way starts in the park at Edale, that walkers' centre supreme, and wastes no time in getting to grips with Kinder Scout, climbs to the Snake Pass and then takes on the waste of Bleaklow, 2,060 ft (633 m), a formidable place in poor weather.

There are even more walking routes in the White

Peak, and the roads are good as country roads go; so transport and foot explorations offer many delightful possibilities. There are excellent viewpoints everywhere. Apart from the attraction of the caverns, there are some easy walks around Castleton and some sublime prospects. Bradwell, to the south east, is a quaint little place too with another popular show cavern, the Bagshawe. Down the A625 is Hathersage, another recommended walking centre. (And here I had to look up one of my folk heroes: Little John's grave is in the churchyard.)

Down at the southern end of the park the valleys are well served with access points and car parks. Some of the village touring centres are especially attractive. I will mention two favourites: strange little Longnor is one, Hartington has to be another. It

But the high land of the Dark Peak is great country for walking, though the groughs complicate route finding and can make the going tougher than expected. The vastness is broken by those distinct features – the broken gritstone edges and the tors. The tors here are of different rock to the weird and intricate sculptures of Dartmoor. Here they look as if put together from a giant construction kit. Full marks though for the masterpieces on the highest land, 2,088 ft (636 m) Kinder Scout. The edges, such as Stanage, Laddow and The Roaches, have produced literally thousands of rock-climbing routes of all grades, and every climber in the country has to have a go on the gritstone at some time or other. In more recent years attention has also turned to the limestone cliffs.

Broomhead Moor, crossed by the Bar Dyke, a mysterious Dark Age earthwork.

Noe Stool, one of the tors on Kinder summit.

The Peak Park's study centre at Losehill Hall provides opportunities for students of all ages to learn about the national park.

Hartington village, dominated by its parish church.

has real style, a model Derbyshire village, and it is close to the twin delectable valleys of the Dove and the Manifold.

The pessimists might suggest that the Peak Park is, or will be, swamped and ruined by its great popularity. But the Park Authority has done a splendid job, especially in holding back the urban spread that would surely have devoured some precious countryside. In 1966 it was the first area to hold the Council of Europe's Conservation Diploma. It has always been innovative. One instance was the

bold decision to introduce traffic management schemes in the Goyt and Upper Derwent valleys, and the opening of the 'Routes for People' traffic scheme in the White Peak area. For years to come it will continue to earn the gratitude of the many who, like I did, will experience that early introduction to real countryside.

The Peak National Park is the supreme oasis in England's heartland. Those who enjoy it have no need to be wary about that desire to return. They will not be disappointed.

Yorkshire
Dales
National Park

Anyone who has lived alongside and worked with Yorkshire people knows that they often fit the traditional image. They are taciturn, unaffected, uncomplicated, pragmatic and thoroughly reliable. Their best talents are often hidden behind the barrier of canny reticence.

I have always felt that the Yorkshire Dales have much of the Yorkshire character. No showy nonsense, but honest to goodness wide-open spaces of green, stippled and striped with white and grey stone; fields webbed with many walls and

Year of designation	1954
Area	680 sq miles (1,761 sq km)
Population	16,842 (1981)
Land use (approx)	
Enclosed farmland	41%
Open country	56%
Commercial forestry	2%
Deciduous woodland	1%
Land ownership	
National Park	0.1%
National Trust	1.3%
Natural areas of special interest	
National Nature Reserves	3
Other nature reserves	6
Sites of Special Scientific Interest	62

Administering authority
Yorkshire Dales National Park Committee,
North Yorkshire County Council,
Yorebridge House,
Bainbridge,
Leyburn, North Yorkshire DL8 3BP
Tel: (0969) 50456
and at
Colvend,
Hebden Road,
Grassington,
Skipton, North Yorkshire BD23 5LB
Tel: (0756) 752748

Most of the park lies within the county of North Yorkshire but 12% is within Cumbria.

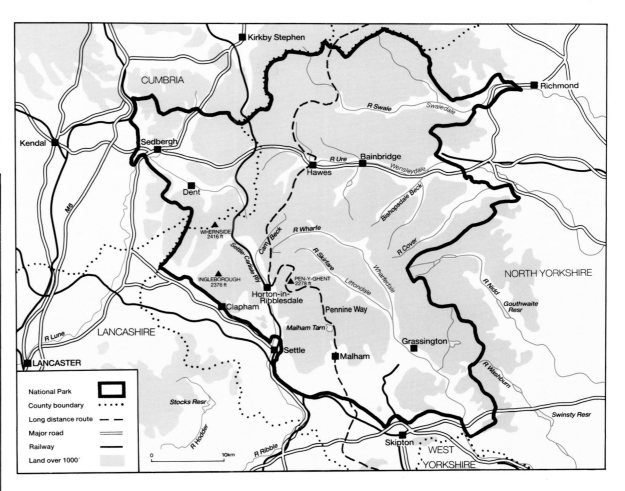

Left:
Yorkshire Dales National Park – a delightful atmosphere of freedom; wide open hills and friendly dales.

dotted with field barns; dark coloured wind-swept moors with heather and moorgrass. It is so open and free that it could be thought that one has the measure of it, only to find, deceptively hidden away in the hollows of the hills and dales, unsuspected treasures of stone hamlets – and many waterfalls, almost at every turn. And hostelries, some with that old-fashioned warm hospitality that went out in other areas with the advent of plastic bars and fast food. This is walking country *par excellence*. But it offers more. It has a delightful atmosphere of freedom. A landscape which expands experience, not at all dramatically, but with captivating subtlety.

The Yorkshire Dales National Park was

Yorkshire Dales National Park.

designated because of its outstanding landscape. It is an area of expansive hill pastures and moorland, most of it above 590 ft (180m), with twenty-nine hill tops above 2,000 ft (610 m) and the well trodden summits of the well known 'Three Peaks': Ingleborough, 2,376 ft (723 m), Pen-y-ghent, 2,278 ft (694 m) and Whernside, 2,416 ft (736 m); and with more than twenty of those genial dales.

It is supreme limestone country, the best in Britain. Its more imposing limestone features – the

Geology of the Yorkshire Dales.

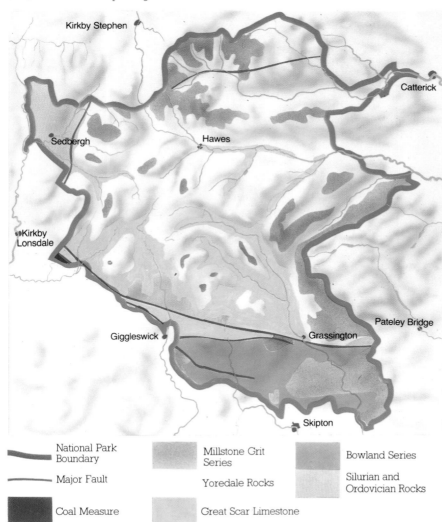

National Park Boundary

Major Fault

Coal Measure

Millstone Grit Series

Yoredale Rocks

Great Scar Limestone

Bowland Series

Silurian and Ordovician Rocks

Malham Cove – cut by ice, trimmed by an ancient waterfall, and now just with a flooded cave at its foot.

Hart's tongue. A fern of limestone grikes.

pavements, cliffs and coves, caves and swallow holes – are much visited by geologists. Malham Cove, with its 985 foot (300 m) wide amphitheatre of 230 ft (70 m) high beetle-browed cliffs, has long become a large open-air classroom, attracting more than 30,000 students each year. Indeed, the whole park is a revealing living textbook of geology and geomorphology.

The limestone of the Yorkshire Dales overlies the earlier folded rocks of the Silurian and Ordovician periods. And in its turn, the north and east has a covering of later shale, sandstones and a limestone, the Yoredale series.

The great mass of white limestone is most visible in the centre and the west of the national park and is known as the 'Great Scar'. The stone makes a major contribution to the unique character of the park. Typical of the limestone country are the upland fells of bright green pasture, criss-crossed with white walls and studded with white-walled field barns. Then there are the spectacular cliffs on the one hand and hill plateaux on the other, with areas of limestone pavement; the surface plates, 'clints' patterned with the deep clefts, 'grikes'. There are very extensive pavements around Ingleborough and across Chapel le Dale on Scales Moor. Here botanists get down on their knees to seek the limestone plants in the grikes which are out of reach of grazing sheep!

There is another feature of such limestone country that is not immediately obvious. Rain and ground water absorbs carbon dioxide to make a weak acid

Buildings in Thwaite, built of the darker stone of the Yoredale series and roofed with stone slabs. The roof pitches are shallow and supported by heavy timbers.

solution which dissolves limestone. Where water descends into natural hollows the rock is gradually eaten away; hence the grikes in the pavement and the extraordinary landform of 'organ pipe' rocks, the 'Buttertubs' on the pass between Hawes and Thwaite. Streams can eventually dissolve their way

to vanish underground. The points where they disappear are known as swallow holes, sink holes, or larger potholes. The streams often reappear from cave mouths in a lower valley.

In between the swallows and the cave mouths, intricate and sometimes very extensive underground passage-ways and caverns can be produced. One cavern below the famous Gaping Gill on Ingleborough is larger than the nave of York Minster. The Dales National Park is famous for its cave systems, and they have been visited since Yordas cave in Kingsdale in the west of the park was 'discovered' by the tourists of the eighteenth century. Since then, White Scar caves near Ingleton, Ingleborough Cave and Stump Cross Caverns by Grassington have been promoted as enjoyable tourist attractions, while the more intrepid adventurers explore the many other cave systems, descending 340 ft (104 m) with a waterfall into Gaping Gill, or Alum Pot near Selside in Ribblesdale. There is still scope for new discoveries by carefully equipped and experienced 'cavers'.

After the formation of the Great Scar limestone more sedimentary rock was formed above it: the Yoredale series. This has been swept away by the glacial ice where the Great Scar limestone is now exposed. However, this Yoredale rock makes a cover over the north of the park. It is very noticeable in Wensleydale. ('Yoredale' is the old name for the valley.) The Yoredale hills are covered typically with coarse pasturage with a darker look to it, the drystone walls in varying shades of grey.

Walkers can see the successive layers of rock as the higher hills are climbed. Eventually on the summits of the Three Peaks and the high land to the north and east there is peat moor, heather, crags and bog. Here is the last and uppermost layer, the Millstone Grit. This rock when weathered is almost black, the walls scoring black lines on the landscape. The Three Peaks stand proud above the high land because, like all prudent outdoor Yorkshiremen, they wear caps – of erosion-resistant Millstone Grit.

Mention must be made again of that older Silurian/Ordovician rock which is not quite entirely overlaid by the Great Scar limestone. This rock consists of ancient mudstones, flags, grits and slate and is exposed where the limestone has been completely worn away by running water. However, there is a major exposure dominant in the west of the park near Sedbergh in the Howgill Fells.

Whatever the rock the nearest examples are those seen immediately in the drystone walls, built of material closest to hand. Transitions can be seen. For instance, travelling from Burnsall to Grassington one is going gradually into limestone country, and the dark walls become mottled as they include limestone rocks; the limestone content gradually increases.

Rocks are the building blocks of landscape, but other factors determine the architecture. Even the hardest rock can become malleable or friable under the enormous weight of natural forces. There are many examples of U-shaped valleys carved out by glaciers. Littondale is a good one. The higher sides of the U are left as long walls of cliffs.

The ice also plucked away at the more yielding rocks to leave the step-like structures on the hill sides. It cut through the intruding spurs of high land to leave exposed crag wounds. Kilnsey Crag is the best example. It is fantastic. The ice chopped off the end to leave a long high cliff towering over the flat valley floor – so distinct and grotesque in outline it looks as if it happened recently. The glaciers often carried plucked-off stone as they moved on, to drop them as they melted. Large boulders of alien

Millstone Grit on the moors near Grassington.

Above right:
Silurian rock of the Howgills with its typically high billowing shapes with few edges.

Chapel-le-Dale, one of the typically U-shaped valleys.

100

greywacke are perched oddly on Great Scar land at Norber on Ingleborough – a textbook feature ('erratics') and a curiosity to the ordinary walker.

As the ice melted it also left behind heaps of debris, including the drumlins which are a feature of Wensleydale. Semer Water was trapped in its valley above Bainbridge by a barrier of debris. The lake was once much larger but became silted. Malham Tarn was scooped out by the ice to an impervious slate level, but this lake too is impounded by a natural dam.

A great feature of the Dales is the very large number of waterfalls, from the spectacular to magical miniatures. Thousands of students, as well as those that appreciate natural beauty, walk from Ingleton, by the lovely wooded way past the Pecca Falls to Thornton Force. A geological trail guide has been provided by the Park's Information Service. The force has a clear fall from a limestone lip of 46 ft (14 m), onto near-vertically bedded Ordovician slates.

On a higher scale there is Hardraw Force near Hawes in Wensleydale. Water here drops an awesome 90 ft (27 m) from the overhanging limestone. A greater series of falls, in volume if not in height, is of course the deservedly popular Aysgarth Falls in Wensleydale. They attract around a million admirers each year. The Park's car park is above on the northern bank and it has a popular visitor centre and cafe.

For height again, if not volume, one needs to go to the north-west of the park, to the north-east of Sedbergh where Cautley Spout spills over Silurian rock into a glacial hollow which probably once held the last lingering volume of ice. The drop is a broken 600 ft (183 m). But all Dales' enthusiasts have their favourite waterfalls; perhaps beautiful rather than spectacular.

For a revelation of the power of moving water without going underground, a visit to Gordale Scar is imperative. This is an incredible piece of natural architecture. Water falls from the high cliffs above through a narrow limestone gorge which is approachable through a cove of overhanging walls. At its upper fall the water spouts through an arch of rock and tumbles over an apron of redeposited limestone (tufa). The shapes of the narrowing gorge above are grotesque. It is possible that this was caused by the enormous amount of moving meltwater flowing from the last ice mass.

In 1838 near Settle an exploring dog is said to

Thornton Force, near Ingleton. Kingsdale Beck cascades over a staircase of horizontal limestone slabs, and then drops clear into the plunge pool in the weaker underlying slate.

have discovered one of the earliest signs of human presence in the Dales when it breached an entrance into the then hidden Victoria Cave. When the cave was cleared of debris, among the bones of prehistoric and later animals was found a barbed harpoon or spearhead made from a deer antler. Human traces of the Mesolithic era have been found in the Dales. They began the clearing of the forest, probably by burning, which was continued more effectively by later Neolithic settlers. Some of these again occupied convenient caves, but used them also for burials and probably for religious purposes. The 'Giant Grave', to the east of the summit of Pen-y-ghent, is one of the relatively few constructed grave sites that one expects to find of this period. There is one clear henge, Castle Dykes high on Aysgarth Moor, reckoned to be late Neolithic/early Bronze Age – it is without standing stones. But why are there no megalithic monuments in the Dales? Were they all destroyed? There was hardly a shortage of material.

Many Iron Age settlements have most probably been built over since, but there are some traces left. The showpiece is the extensive remains of the large hillfort which crowns Ingleborough and contains traces of hut circles. 'Maiden Castle' at the east end of Swaledale may have been a chieftain's base, and there are more, puzzling earthworks not far away at Grinton.

There are clear traces of Roman occupation at Bainbridge (*Virosidum*) in the form of foundations of a fort. The Romans were certainly in the area to collect lead, for lead pigs with Roman markings have been found, but any signs of Roman mining will have been destroyed by later activity.

Crosses and tombs are evidence of Norse and Anglo Saxon settlement. In the medieval period much of the park area was in the ownership of abbeys and priories, notably the wealthy Fountains Abbey. Some of the higher lands were hunting preserves.

Visitors will doubtless wish to visit the castles at Richmond and Skipton, which are outside the park. Middleham Castle, just beyond the eastern boundary, had a great bearing on the Dales for it was the home of Richard of Gloucester, later Richard III. Richard was not a saint, but he was not the hunchbacked villain that Tudor propagandists would have us believe, either. He was a man of Wensleydale so he could not be all bad! He did much for the economy of the Dales and commanded

The Roman road linking *Virosidum* via Ingleton to Lancaster, with Semer Water below.

a great deal of loyalty in the area. There are still dalesmen who will hear no ill of him.

The only castle ruin within the park is Bolton Castle, just six miles (10 km) from Middleham as the crow flies. It must be seen, for here lived Richard's loyal neighbours, the Scropes. This is no town castle. It is isolated in its own estate, which is now a working agricultural landscape. The structure is stark and seems to have grown naturally from the rock on which it stands. It is difficult now to imagine that this was once the scene of courtly elegance. It was built in the late fourteenth century by Richard le

Scrope, who served as Lord Chancellor to Richard II. The castle took its place in history when Henry, the ninth Lord Scrope, was the able and respected law Warden of the Scottish border's Western March between 1563 and 1590. It was during this tenure that Mary Queen of Scots, threatened by her enemies at home, fled to England to be detained at Carlisle Castle. Scrope thought that this was too near the intrigues of the border for comfort and had her brought to Bolton Castle. It was during her six months stay that the Commission of York was making enquiries about her possible involvement in her husband's death, and the 'Casket Letters' (forgeries?) were produced. It was also here that her correspondence with the Duke of Norfolk

The quarries have supplied sandstones, pavement flags and roofing slates as well as limestone. Many quarries are abandoned and colonised by vegetation, but some are still active and making an important contribution to the local economy. The hundreds of old limestone kilns in the park are evidence of the long known value of lime for agriculture and building. However, there is a vast difference between the traditional way of quarrying to supply local needs and the modern way when technology vastly increases production from the quarries while minimising on manpower; it is questionable whether the benefits justify the cost to the environment. Why should high quality limestone be quarried in vast quantities to be wasted as aggregate? The scars of limestone quarries can be horrendous. This is a headache that the National Park Authority shares with the Peak District National Park. The noise and the dust clouds and the large number of heavy vehicles using the narrow roads are further problems. A national park in Britain is a living landscape and as such has to be accepted 'warts and all'. Scars were there long before the park was designated. But scars should not become running sores. The Park Authority has to try, through the exercise of planning control, to minimise future impact.

Farming, the pasturing of sheep and cattle, has been the traditional industry of the Dales since Neolithic times. It has given the Dales its colour,

occurred and was intercepted by Sir Francis Walsingham (surely the founder of MI5?). There is much of the ruin to see, though the additional work planned will help to make a visit more rewarding.

The ruined Bolton Priory (in lower Wharfedale, nowhere near Bolton Castle!), was an Augustinian priory praised by both Wordsworth and Ruskin for its beauty, which should be enough to put it high on the visitor's itinerary. It will be no disappointment. Its position, in placid green fields by the river, is superb and unforgettable and there is much enjoyable public access around it. The priory is not large, but although the roof was taken down from all but the nave at the Dissolution there is much of the lovely structure to see. It was founded in 1154 on a site which was a gift of Cecily de Rumilley. The ruin, currently being made more safe, has most walls standing to the original height. The eye is drawn to the elegant arch of the east window but it is a pity that the stone tracery has gone.

Up dale from the priory is Barden Tower, a massive fifteenth century tower house built by Henry Clifford, loyal supporter of Richard III. His wealth at the time had much to do with the development of lead mining on Grassington Moor. Today there is evidence of old lead mining activity in many places in the Dales, particularly in the north of the park. There are concentrations around Arkengarthdale and in Wharfedale.

Quarrying is a traditional industry in the Dales.

Bolton Priory ruins. The nave was saved as a parish church at the Dissolution. All is thirteenth and fourteenth century. The west front is a masterpiece.

Barden Tower. Restored by the indefatigable Lady Anne Clifford in the seventeenth century and now a picturesque ruin.

Working Quarries

▲ Limestone

▲ Greywacke

Old Mines and Quarries

● Lead

● Zinc

◆ Coal

▲ Grit

◢ Flagstone

■ Limestone

◣ Slate

Mines and quarries within the park area.

field barns can fall into disrepair. If walls fall, a fence can be easily erected in its place. The whole character of the park can be transformed. The National Park Authority is aware of the need to work closely with its farmers. The EEC now has a regulation enabling payments to be available to help farmers to farm in the traditional methods in 'Environmentally Sensitive Areas'. On the advice of

Old Gang Smelt Mill remains, conserved by the Park under a management agreement. Lead mining took place in the Dales from Roman times until the nineteenth century.

'Traditional' hay making in Swaledale.

Opposite:
The pattern of traditional farming in Wharfedale. The Park Authority's policy is to help the farmer to keep his barns and walls in repair. Grant aid has enabled some barns to be converted to bunkhouse accommodation.

texture and magic. One of the captivating features is the pattern of walled hay meadows scattered with the colour of spring flowers, a sight that can still be enjoyed. However, times can change. To survive nowadays the hill farmer is drawn towards more intensive farming methods. Fertilisers and herbicides can help to produce a wealth of uniformly green grass and machines can take the place of human hands. When no longer needed,

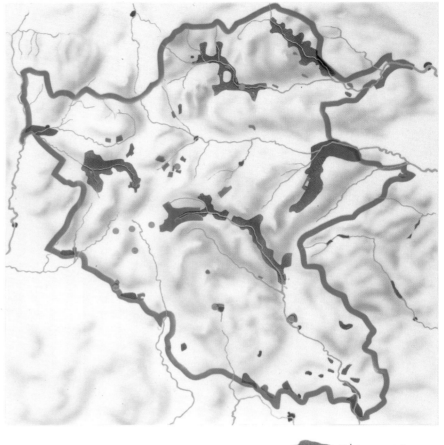

Broadleaf Woodland	Open Water	Environmentally Sensitive Area
Conifer Forest	Nature Reserve	Grade 3 Farmland

the National Park Authority, the Countryside Commission and the Nature Conservancy Council, parts of Dentdale, Deepdale, Swaledale, Arkengarthdale, Walden, Wharfedale and Langstrothdale have been included in the 'Pennine Dales' Environmentally Sensitive Area. Although it is voluntary, there is optimism on the outcome of this innovative scheme which encourages farmers to conserve this valuable landscape.

Another great example of human economic

Natural history and conservation. Notable features are limestone flora – a nature reserve in Wharfedale has 400 species – and fine herb-rich hay meadows.

activity came to the Dales in the nineteenth century. The Settle to Carlisle railway line is a happy celebration of determined engineering along its whole length. Although threatened with closure, it has the affection and respect of many. Loyalty fostered by the National Park's 'Dales Rail' promotion in 1975, and support from local authorities, has ensured that it has existed through the 1980s. Although carrying more passengers now than for many years, its future is still uncertain and in the end will depend on the private sector's willingness to take it on. The Park has a programme of guided walks starting from some of the stations.

The line from Settle serves Horton-in-Ribblesdale, Ribblehead, and Dent. Horton-in-Ribblesdale is a pretty village overshadowed by the great quarry; but it is a centre for walkers and cavers with access to the Three Peaks. For reasons best known to themselves, some walkers and runners do this route in one day. Dent, in delectable Dentdale, has cobbled streets and a decent, neat, scrubbed-clean atmosphere, like a Dales dame off to Sunday chapel. Adam Sedgwick (1785–1873) was born here. He became the 'father of geology' and was a respected Cambridge professor. A boulder of Shap granite is his memorial. These are only two of the little settlements that are the essential attractions in the Dales. All have long served the scattered farming communities, also housing the craftsmen and the miners. Here are the shops, the church and the school. No neat and smug thatched cottages, but all businesslike local stone. There is little space here to mention more than a few places which are worth a visit.

Probably the best known dale in the park is Wharfedale. Grassington, once a busy miners' town, is now the bustling centre of Wharfedale, with some old houses and cobbled ways. The National Park's administrative offices are here, as well as a busy Visitor Information Centre. Kettlewell is the superb show village of Wharfedale. It is in a conservation area and can be very crowded at weekends and holidays. It is an ideal holiday centre with some of the Dales' best features in the area, such as fields criss-crossed with walls, and the high lines of crags hemming the glaciated valley. Burnsall, a handsome place in lower Wharfedale, has a five-arched bridge over the river. The church has a Norse hog-back tombstone and Norse/Saxon cross. Eleven graves of this period were found in the churchyard, which has an intriguing

A special train crosses Ribblehead Viaduct, which has twenty-four arches, the tallest 165 ft (50 m) high.

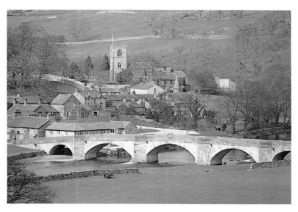

Burnsall by the River Wharfe.

seventeenth century self-adjusting turnstile. Near the junction of Wharfedale with Langstrothdale is Buckden. This was once a medieval hunting lodge. Nearby Buckden Pike is where lead was mined.

West of Wharfedale is Arncliffe in Littondale, a favourite gem with its typical village green. Little St Oswald church has a list of local Dalesmen, bowmen and billmen, who fought at Flodden Field. A bill is hung on a wall, making it seem only a little time ago. To the south is the sublime, handsome village of Malham, one of the most visited in the park. A place to have one a-tingle with anticipation for nearby Malham Cove, Malham Tarn and Gordale Scar, with waterfalls and walks galore.

On the southern park boundary in Ribblesdale is Settle, a great little market town. It is a tradition of my family that Christmas hospitality is sampled here when the place is gay with coloured lights and warm with friendship. It is a good walking centre for the park with an excellent museum run by the North Craven Heritage Trust. North-west along the A65 is Clapham, a picturesque Dales village arranged round Clapham Beck, and a good access point for Ingleborough with its well appointed Park Visitor Centre. Further along the A65 is Ingleton, an unashamed small town tourist centre with all that that means good and blatant, but it is a first class base for geologists, botanists, cavers and walkers, and the hungry and thirsty. There is access from here to the fine walk to Thornton Force.

Sedbergh is a little town on the western edge of the park. Its geology and direct line of communication to Kendal are Cumbrian, but it has the full flavour of a Dales village with welcoming

Left:
The River Clough in Garsdale.

shops, narrow streets and alleyways leading to the fell.

Hawes is the market town of Wensleydale, with a wide market street. Duerly Beck makes an impressive commotion as it drops down its rocky bed and under the bridge. The Park Visitor Centre is at the old railway station. The famous Hardraw Force waterfall is to the north-west. Hawes is also a popular refreshment centre for walkers on the Pennine Way. East along the A684 is Bainbridge on the river Bain which flows from not-so-far away Semer Water and makes a pretty fall by the bridge which gives the village its name. There is a large village green and traces of the Roman fort, *Virosidum*, on the hill to the east.

In lovely Upper Swaledale is the little village of Muker with its grey houses and walled fields scattered around as if dropped by a careless giant. A small neighbouring settlement to Muker, containing the whole essence of the higher dales, is Thwaite. An away-from-it-all walking centre of which dreams are made. The pass over to Hawes by the quaint Buttertubs starts nearby. Reeth is a little, friendly Swaledale centre with its buildings sitting around a village green. It has an almost alpine

A lone walker on the hill by Ingleborough.

Evening sun and the first touch of autumn colour are a lovely combination for a stand of broadleaf trees in a gulley in Coverdale.

Reconstructed steps and path at Malham Cove replace eroded scars.

atmosphere. Lead mining was its making and the excellent folk museum tells all. High up at 1,100 feet by the Pennine Way in Upper Swaledale is Keld, a no-nonsense hamlet. This is what it is all about! A walker's paradise.

However, the Yorkshire Dales National Park is not without its problems. Some can be effectively solved in time. The key to the public enjoyment of all that the park has to offer is a well-maintained footpath system. There are some 1,067 miles (1,717 km) of public rights of way in the park and it is crossed by a 57 mile (85 km) section of the Pennine Way long distance footpath. The immense and growing popularity of hill walking produces its severe erosion toll on vulnerable high-level surfaces, particularly on peat. Remedial work is under way on a major restoration project on the Three Peaks, funded by the National Park Authority, the Countryside Commission and the Nature Conservancy Council. The project has to ensure that the restoration blends totally with the terrain, and somehow devastated areas must be recolonised with vegetation.

The eighteenth century Whernside Manor is the National Park Authority's own Outdoor Study and Recreation Centre in Dentdale where regular courses are organised or, by arrangement, groups can do their own thing. There are six National Park Visitor Centres, and eighteen village information points in shops and post offices, with information display boards at many sites around the park. The Information Service exists to help the visitor get the fullest enjoyment from an exploration of the many treasures of the Yorkshire Dales.

North York
Moors
National Park

Expansive views are the supreme offering of the North York Moors National Park, for it occupies a great bulk of high land up to 1,400 ft (427 m) above the rich vale of York lying to its south, with the plain of the Tees to its north. The North Sea washes the cliffs on its eastern boundary. This upland area is criss-crossed with roads, tracks and paths, many of them very ancient and offering stupendous prospects. The other seductive attraction is the far-stretching spread of heather, offering an amazing sight in late summer's bloom. The heather moors here are more continuous and extensive than in any

Year of designation	1952
Area	553 sq miles (1,432 sq km)
Population	25,253 (1981)
Land use (approx)	
Enclosed farmland	42%
Open country	35%
Commercial forestry	18%
Deciduous woodland	5%
Land ownership (approx)	
National Park	2%
Forestry Commission	16.5%
Water Authority	0.1%
National Trust	1.25%
Natural areas of special interest	
National Nature Reserves	1
Other nature reserves	8
Sites of Special Scientific Interest	38

Administering authority
North York Moors National Park Committee,
North Yorkshire County Council,
The Old Vicarage,
Bondgate,
Helmsley,
York,
Y06 5BP
Tel: (0439) 70657

The national park is mainly in the county of North Yorkshire, with a small proportion in the county of Cleveland.

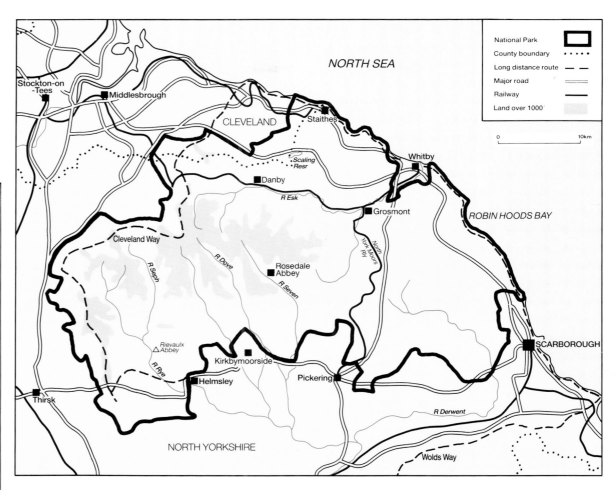

Left:
North York Moors National Park – rolling, flowing, billowing countryside with wide horizons.

other part of England and Wales. Even when the heather is not in full bloom it adds much to the changing moods, colour and texture of the moors. The contrast is in the green of the deep dales that are scooped out of this landscape. They are generally much wider and less confined than those of the Yorkshire Dales.

The North York Moors is the easternmost of the national parks, and because of this it has a drier and somewhat cooler climate than that of the other parks. It also has the youngest rocks, since the base rocks are of the Jurassic period, a mere 195–145 million years old. Jurassics are normally classified into three periods: the lower, middle and upper.

North York Moors National Park.

They vary from the lower liassic shales, through sandstone, clay, grit and limestone. The whole was folded by earth movements and as it was lifted from the sea it was eroded. The area was covered by the slow moving glaciers of the early Ice Ages moving from Scotland and the Lake District. Melt waters caused further erosion by overflowing down from lakes and gouging out gorges and valleys which exist to this day.

There is some dramatic evidence that there was animal life in this area between the ice movements. In the pretty vale of Kirkdale, east of Helmsley, when roadstone was being extracted from a quarry in 1821 a cave was broken into revealing a large collection of animal bones (now on display at the Yorkshire Museum in York). They were subsequently identified as including animals from sub-tropical to cool climate species: rhino, lion, tiger, bear, elephant and giant deer. The preponderance of hyena bones on upper layers suggests that the cave was inhabited by hyenas which dragged in the other carcasses. Alas the cave was quarried away and only quarry-wall slits from the back of the cave remain to be seen now in a little bird-loud wood.

There were no human bones in the cave. Hunter-fishermen of the old and middle Stone Ages must have used the area, but as in other regions it was the coming of the Neolithic culture with superior tools which began to make a human mark on the landscape. The agriculturalists needed to make clearings in the forest by axe and fire, evidence of this being shown in core samples taken from the moorland peat. The pollen identified showed that around 8000 BC the area was covered in forest; but later, coinciding with Neolithic/Bronze Age settlement, there was a change towards grassland and heather. Bronze Age settlement became very extensive from around 2000 BC. Grazing domestic animals prevented the regeneration of the forest and the soil on the hilltops began to be impoverished. The extent of the human settlements can be seen in the scattering of burial mounds throughout the whole region. Tumuli and cairns (sometimes 'Howes') are shown everywhere on the map. Some of the larger mounds crown high points such as the one on Danby Beacon. Most have been excavated and found to contain bones and pottery. However, a significant one on Loose Howe, a high point on the moors between Rosedale and Danby Dale, contained a body in a 'coffin' of a canoe with

Geological section. The rocks of The North York Moors were laid down as sediments during Jurassic times between about 210 and 145 million years ago. The section A – B across the moors from the Vale of Pickering to the North Sea shows clearly the three layers of Lower, Middle and Upper Jurassic rocks and the effects of erosion which have given the national park landscape its distinctive characteristics.

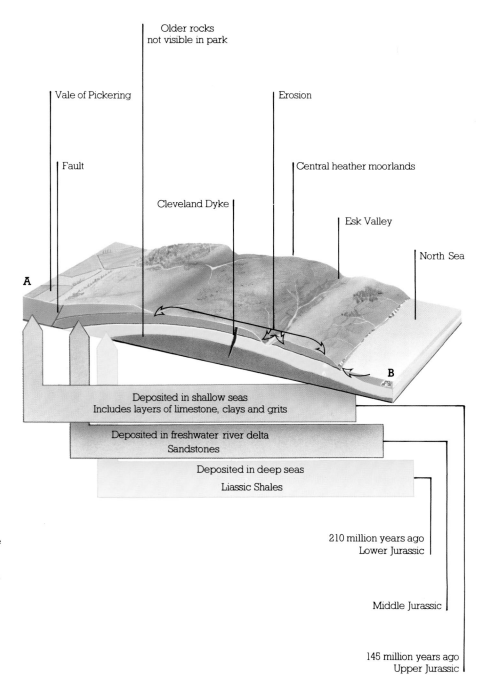

Older rocks not visible in park

Vale of Pickering

Erosion

Fault

Central heather moorlands

Cleveland Dyke

Esk Valley

North Sea

A

B

Deposited in shallow seas
Includes layers of limestone, clays and grits

Deposited in freshwater river delta
Sandstones

Deposited in deep seas
Liassic Shales

210 million years ago
Lower Jurassic

Middle Jurassic

145 million years ago
Upper Jurassic

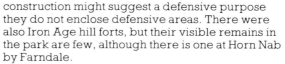

A burial mound tops the high point of Danby Beacon.

construction might suggest a defensive purpose they do not enclose defensive areas. There were also Iron Age hill forts, but their visible remains in the park are few, although there is one at Horn Nab by Farndale.

The Romans left little trace of their occupation. There are remains of a Roman encampment at Cawthorne by the park's southern boundary. This site with its unique square compounds is now owned by the National Park, who are establishing interpretive trails. A splendid section of Roman road foundations has been uncovered at the eastern end of Wheeldale Moor, now in the care of English Heritage. There were Roman signal stations on the coast at Goldsborough, Huntcliffe and Ravenscar. Only the foundations of the first site are now barely recognisable.

When King Edwin of Northumberland was converted, Celtic and later Saxon missionaries came into the area and built their chapels. Whitby was the site of one Saxon minster and another was founded by the Celts at Lastingham, north-east of Kirkby Moorside. The former was overbuilt by a medieval abbey, but Lastingham? A pilgrimage to St Mary's church at Lastingham is recommended. Although the church has seen much change, what it contains is quite unique. The Venerable Bede recorded the establishment of a monastery in this 'wild' place by St Cedd and St Chad in 659. It was burned by the Danes and replaced later by another structure when Stephen, Abbot of Whitby, asked leave of King William I to rebuild the monastery. He did not finish it as he apparently found the area inhospitable and moved on to build the abbey of St Mary's at York.

another canoe acting as lid. A third canoe was also enclosed. With the body was a skin cloak, a knife, shoes and leggings; all are now in the British Museum.

One would expect to see stone circles of the period, however none remain in their entirety, though of the many standing stones on the moor some go back into far antiquity. There is one henge circle in the park, Studford Ring, north of Ampleforth. This consists of an outer embankment and inner ditch enclosing a flat area about 165 ft (50 m) in diameter. If there were stones here they have now gone. Nearby are dykes; indeed ancient linear earthworks are everywhere in the park and there are few clues to their use. They are surely too elaborate as boundary markers, and though their

The foundations of the Roman road on Wheeldale Moor.

The extraordinary Norman crypt in St Mary's church at Lastingham.

St Gregory's Minster, Kirkdale.

The monastic settlements had a great influence in the moors. They continued the opening up of the forest and brought their wealth-producing flocks of sheep. Thirteenth century Whitby abbey's ruined church, seen against the sky on its high headland from many parts of the moor (in some views marred by the proximity of a tall sacrilegious aerial!), was a Benedictine foundation. But within the park there are abbey church ruins of great beauty. No one can visit Rievaulx in the dale of the Rye, which gave it its name, and be unmoved. Enhanced by its setting in the wooded valley it can surely only be rivalled by Tintern. In some lights its pale sandstone shines like gold. J M W Turner painted and sketched the scene with obvious care, a work which can be seen in the Tate Gallery. This was the first large Cistercian church in Britain. The abbey was founded in the twelfth century on land gifted by Walter l'Espec, and by the latter part of the century the whole of the monastic buildings were completed. Under Abbot Ailred (1147–1167) it is recorded that the abbey had 140 monks and at least 500 lay brothers.

Because of the tight restrictions of the site the church was exceptionally aligned north to south.

Twelfth century Rievaulx Abbey seen from the terrace.

However, what he did leave was made into a chapel in 1228 from what would have been the east end of a large abbey church. Four great pillars are part of the structure. But the intensely moving revelation is below – in the crypt. To find a crypt at all in such a little church is extraordinary. But this one, with its sturdy pillars and arches, has remained untouched since it was built by the monks as a shrine to St Cedd in 1078! Stone fragments in the crypt include part of a huge ninth century crosshead which would have been 5 ft in size. The cross shaft which held it would have been 24 ft (7.3 m) high!

Some of the medieval churches contain Saxon stones. A notable example in a cosy wooded setting is in Kirkdale near the quarry of the hyena cave referred to earlier. Here is St Gregory's Minster, a tiny church which some also claim as being founded by St Cedd. But it is part eleventh century Saxon and part twelfth and thirteenth century Norman, with nineteenth century additions. Old pre-Norman cross shafts are built into the walls. But the remarkable feature is within the nineteenth century porch. Casts have been made from it for display in the Science Museum at South Kensington and other museums, for it is the best preserved Saxon sundial in existence.

The Ionic temple on Rievaulx Terrace.

The innovative large nave was built between 1135 and 1140 with nine bays and with aisles on either side. The transepts were of the same date. Beyond, the Gothic masterpiece of Quire and Presbytery with seven bays was added around 1230. The chapter house, where a daily reading of a chapter from the rule of St Benedict was read to remind the monks of their vows and obligations, is separated from the church by the vestry library.

One can sit in the old cloister area and absorb the atmosphere. When Dorothy Wordsworth was here with William on their way to Scarborough to collect William's future bride, she wrote: 'thrushes were singing – hillocks were scattered over with grovelets of wild roses and other shrubs and covered with wild flowers. I could have stayed in this solemn quiet spot till evening without a thought of leaving.'

A serpentine terrace high above the ruins was made on the hillside by the abbey's eighteenth century owner Thomas Duncombe, when the taste for romantic landscapes and Gothic ruins was the height of fashion. He built an Ionic temple at one end of the terrace, a Tuscan one at the other. All now beautifully preserved by the present owners, the National Trust. Viewpoints through the gaps in the trees reveal unforgettable airy views of the abbey ruins.

Only two miles away from Rievaulx is Old Byland where there were the beginnings of another abbey. It was founded by monks of the Order of Savigny who had abandoned an abbey in Cumbria after it had been sacked by the Scots. They were only there for four years because the abbeys could hear each other's bells by day and night which 'could by no means be endured'. They had to move. The little church dedicated to St Oswald is a fragment of what the monks left at Old Byland, in a handsome little village fronted by a village green. It contains many signs of the monks' early stonework.

The monks set off on their wanderings again, during which time their Order was absorbed into the Cistercians. In 1177 they settled on the existing site of Byland Abbey by the southernmost boundary of the park. Its remains, though far more ruinous and quarried than Rievaulx's, are quite beautiful and must be seen. Immediately striking, with its one tower above the broken wheel window, the church's west front looks like a great hand pointing to heaven. The church's large nave compares with Rievaulx's. Parts of the original green and yellow tiled floors are preserved. Stone fragments show that the church interior was at one time painted red and white.

The site museum shows examples of the superior craftsmanship in stone carving, particularly of the capitals and corbels of the abbey church. Two curiosities on show found in the ruins are the abbot's inkstand, and a monk's gaming stone for playing 'nine men's morris'.

On the westernmost boundary of the park near Osmotherley, below lovely woodlands, are the ruins of the relatively small Mount Grace Priory founded in 1398 by the Carthusian Order. A light tower rises above the remaining walls of the church nave. The order believed in isolation and fifteen cells round the cloister housed fifteen solitary monks. Five more cells were later added by the south court.

The other formidable relics of medieval times, of course, are the castles. Scarborough's famous castle, and Pickering's, are outside the park. But if Helmsley is approached from the east or south one cannot fail to be impressed by the remnant of its great castle keep rising above the town. Its building was begun by Robert de Roos, Lord of Helmsley from 1186 to 1227. The west range of domestics are

well preserved as it was occupied until the eighteenth century. The keep received its drastic damage in the Civil War when the castle was held by Sir Jordan Crosland for the king, and taken after a three month's seige, by Sir Thomas Fairfax.

Helmsley itself is a favourite little market town of attractive buildings. The River Rye runs under its bridge, and a stream runs through the town centre. Were the areas now covered by tarmac roads once a village green? First impressions often linger. To me the place suggests 'mellow fruitfulness' for, on an early visit when the gardens were at their best in perfect autumn weather, a barrel filled with apples stood outside one of the houses. By it was a notice 'Help yourself'. I ate one of the most crisp and delicious apples I have ever tasted and remembered that Dorothy Wordsworth recorded too that she rejoiced in the town's hospitality. Helmsley is the capital of the park for it is home to the administrative offices of the National Park Authority.

It is also a good centre for an exploration of the south of the park. Ryedale with its abbey is in easy reach. Westwards the A170 climbs by Scawton Moor to Sutton Bank where the National Park has a Visitor Centre on the edge of the escarpment of the Hambleton Hills. The approach to this spot from Thirsk, way below in the valley, is up a notorious mile-long, winding, one-in-four hill climb; though it is a somewhat humbling experience to watch cyclists in the International Milk Race actually pedalling their way over the summit!

The prospect from this top is remarkable; over 90 miles (145 km) on a clear day. Below the bank can be seen the park's largest natural lake, Lake Gormire, and northwards stretch the Hambleton Hills. Going over the length, Ryedale on the right looks to be in a great hole 700 ft (213 m) below. North of the Hambletons and curving round eastwards and then northwards are the Cleveland Hills with the oddly shaped and named Roseberry Topping, 1,015 ft (309 m), another famous viewpoint which reduces Middlesbrough to its proper place and has the sight and scent of the sea.

A road runs from Guisborough below the Topping and over some of the finest and evocative areas of the moor. Continuing south-eastwards it goes through Westerdale at the top end of the River Esk. The hamlet is just one of the many settlements which enhance the moorland experience. Houses here and in most other places are built of sandstone

Bransdale. Green field patterns fill the valley below the moorland.

Loft Upper floor
Door to cross passage
Cellar
Purlin
Collar beam
Saddle
Ridge Tree
Fireplace and bread oven
Crucks
Tie beam
Bar parlour
Seat
Base stone
Cruck built into large stones at base of wall
Lath covered with lime plaster with horsehair
Plan of walls
Dispense
Lower parlour

with varying subtle shades from pale yellow to deep orange. Climbing on beyond the Esk one hub of the moor is reached where Westerdale and Danby High Moors meet. There are a fair number of crosses on the moor. Here are the Ralph crosses; the 'Young Ralph' nearest the crossroads. Travellers were once expected to leave a coin on the top for the passing poor to collect. To the south-east towards Rosedale Moor is another popular landmark, the corpulant cross 'Fat Betty'; her nakedness is traditionally covered with whitewash.

North of the Cleveland Hills is that great valley of the Esk, ideally savoured perhaps from a railway carriage on the picturesque Esk Valley rural line between Middlesbrough and Whitby. Eskdale is a wide spread of a valley with no feeling of enclosure like the valleys of other parks. Castleton though, a village near its head, has the hint of the alpine about it with many houses scattered this way and that as if sulking and not willing to speak to each other. Castleton's castle cannot be seen. Eskdale once had a castle at Danby, the remains of which are now a farm and not open to the public. They are on the south-east of the village beyond the strangely-named medieval 'Duck Bridge'. The castle was owned by the Nevilles of Raby, and Katherine Parr once lived here as a widow of a Danby Latimer. She married Henry VIII in 1543 and (uniquely) survived him. Tradition has it that Henry visited the castle to see her.

The National Park has a haven nearby; the Moors Centre at Danby Lodge. It was a nineteenth century shooting lodge but now provides information, lectures and refreshments, and is situated on

'Young' Ralph Cross marks the road covered by snow.

Above right:
The interior of Spout House, which is one of the oldest buildings in the park, renovated with the help of the National Park Authority.

Duck Bridge, over the Esk at Danby.

Danby Lodge, the National Park's Moors Centre.

thirteen acres of Eskdale land. Up above Danby on Danby High Moor is another favourite viewpoint, Danby Beacon.

Down dale from Danby, wrapped in woodlands, are the handsome villages of Leaholm and Glaisdale, where one can see the very old packhorse bridge, 'Beggar's Bridge'. Down valley again is Grosmont, the junction between the Esk Valley railway and the North Yorkshire Moors Railway. Hard to imagine now that this rural village was once a thriving industrial centre with three blast furnaces in full spate in the latter half of the nineteenth century, for hereabouts iron was mined in great quantity. A display at the station explains all. Southwards from Grosmont is the valley of the Murk Esk and through it runs the North Yorkshire Moors Railway, on a delectable moorland route, eventually going through forest in Newtondale to Pickering, a route that can only be followed by rail. The line was dis-owned by British Rail and was taken over by enthusiasts, the North Yorkshire Moors Historical Railway Trust, and the line now runs steam trains in the summer season. On Friday and Saturday evenings between May and October one can dine in the North Yorkshire Pullman! The line is deservedly one of the great attractions of the park and the moorland stops are good walking centres.

A view from the Moors Centre.

First stop on the line south from Grosmont is Goathland, also accessible by a moorland road past old iron diggings. This is another attractive stone village among trees. Mallyan Spout, a pretty 70 foot (21 m) waterfall is nearby. A rewarding walk is north by the village of Beck Hole to Grosmont, taking a train for the return journey.

North-east of Helmsley are several dales. Farndale is famous in spring for its great masses of daffodils. East of the lower reach is Hutton-le-Hole, a superb gem of a village with a long village green. A stream runs through and green hummocks are set about it, all well manicured. In this village is the Ryedale Folk Museum, with a famous collection of farm implements, tools and reconstructed buildings. The museum tells the story of the Rosedale iron industry.

Rosedale is the next valley to the east. Its village is at Rosedale Abbey. The Cistercian abbey was dissolved totally after the Dissolution, and clues of the extensive iron workings (1850–1920) have to be sought: such as the extraordinary route of the old

A replica of a sixteenth century manor house at Ryedale Folk Museum.

railway which served it, and the kilns where ironstone was reduced before being transported out of the valley.

From Rosedale there is a choice of moorland roads. The roads criss-crossing the moor are often narrow, and some unbelievably steep. Obviously great care, patience and courtesy to other road users are needed in their negotiation.

One main road, the A169 from Pickering to Whitby, climbs the moor by the Tabular Hills. It passes the odd physical feature known as the Hole of

Horcum, a deep hollow eroded by ages of flowing water. This area with Lockton High Moor to the north, is the property of the Park Authority. Since the park was designated a quarter of the moorland has been lost to forestry and intensive farming practices. The Park's land is held for its protection and as a means to test moorland management

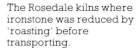

The Rosedale kilns where ironstone was reduced by 'roasting' before transporting.

A part of the great show of daffodils in Farndale.

techniques – for instance, the conservation of heather moorland requires periodical controlled burning.

One can be excused for having mixed feelings when continuing northwards past Ministry of Defence land (their holding is around 2,000 acres/8000 ha) and a view of the Fylingdales Early Warning Station's enormous 'golf balls'. These are to be replaced – by a pyramid.

Further north there is a good view of Whitby and the shore line on the descent to Sleights. All the moorland deserves exploration. Not all of it is heather; there is grassland and bog, and alas a lot of bracken. Peatland left to itself here and there is colonised by birch, Scots pine, gorse and broom. But the views are everything – in all directions, over the up-and-down, rolling, flowing, billowing convolutions of the land; with the sky as companion and the sea as neighbour!

The south-eastern part of the park beyond Pickering is much blanketed with conifer forest. The Forestry Commission, which owns some $16\frac{1}{2}$ per cent of the park, makes amends by offering car parks, picnic areas and trails. The more attractive broadleaved and mixed woodlands supporting a much greater variety of wildlife and plants are scattered throughout the park, sometimes in only small parcels. They cover only 5 per cent of the land

Bell heather

Ling heather

area. To encourage the management of the woodlands and the planting of more broadleaved trees, the Park Authority has tree planting and woodland management schemes.

There is everything in the park that a walker needs with 1,100 miles (1,770 km) of public rights of way, which are maintained by the Park's rangers and outdoor staff. The Information Service's literature suggests where walks can be enjoyed. The Cleveland Way, the great long-distance footpath around the high land of the park, is 93 miles (149 km) in all. It gives opportunity to explore the 25 miles (40 km) of the Heritage Coast which takes up the north-eastern boundary of the park (but

Controlled rotational burning of the heather is a necessary conservation measure.

excludes Whitby and Scarborough). A whole scenic variety of surprise and drama! After going over its moorland highpoints, the route goes east and over Boulby Head, 660 ft (200 m); the highest sea cliffs in eastern England. It continues down the coast to some favourite places. First there is the fishing village of Staithes with three-storey buildings facing each other across the cobbles of the main street – but it is more impressive nearer to the sea, with passages and alleyways. A real little port with lifeboat house and 'cobles', the traditional small fishing boats. At this place James Cook, later the famous Captain Cook, got his first job as a shop assistant before being apprenticed to Captain Sanderson at Whitby and starting a sea career

Beck Hole on the Historical Railway Trail, one of many paths available to walkers.

which led to landings on Australia and New Zealand.

Further still and there is another picturesque steep-sided coastal village at Runswick Bay, with houses all atop of each other and a pleasant sandy beach. A longer beach further on at Sandsend gets crowded at times, being so near the A174. Whitby, next, is outside the park, but it is a very fine hospitable town and small port, held in great affection by many.

One then comes to, arguably, the finest coastal village of all, Robin Hood's Bay (with the reservation that being so superb and small it gets over-full at peak holiday times). Here, on the steep slope, is a maze of steps and alleyways and delightful cottages, so close across the cobbled streets that one could almost shake hands from door to door. Indeed one would need to get on well with neighbours, being so close together – sharing the common hazards of the sea would knit the past community. Some of the village is disappearing under the waves, for the coast has been eroding since the land rose from the sea. All buildings here are in that delightful warm stone, characteristically dressed by the masons in herring-bone pattern.

Robin Hood's Bay is much visited by geologists. The beach and the crumbling cliffs reveal several layers of Jurassic shales. On my earliest visit here

Arctic tern, common tern and sandwich tern: Sandsend is an excellent summer observation post for these sea birds.

'Cobles', traditional fishing boats, at Staithes.

my guide pointed out that a familiar visitor from my home county had beaten me to the place, by some twenty thousand years – a boulder of unmistakable pink granite had come piggy-back all the way on the glacial ice from Shap. If one can be persuaded to leave this great place the Cleveland Way continues and climbs high to Ravenscar where there was a Roman signal station, and continues along airy cliffs, the wrinkled sea below with Scarborough ahead.

The Park Authority with its small dedicated staff has large problems. With all the other national parks it must share a concern for the future of hill

Kittiwakes breed on coastal cliffs.

farming, for nearly half the park is in agricultural use. Practical assistance is given to the farmers by an upland management service, and a number of grant-aid schemes are available to help with farm conservation, woodland management and tree planting, amongst other activities. The Authority also has a moorland management programme, for the heather moors cannot be conserved without active care and the co-operation of all land users. That must include the many visitors who come to share its great beauty.

An unmetalled by-way makes ideal walking across the moors.

Lake District National Park

Since the Lake District's 'discovery' by the artists, poets and writers of the eighteenth and nineteenth centuries it has been a rich source of inspiration for multitudes of enthusiasts. Its instant attraction defies explanation. It is incomparable. Scottish highlands? The scale is far too modest; it could be lost in the Great Glen. Snowdonia? The mountain scene lacks the more aggressive challenge of the Welsh.

It is as if in the 880 square miles of Britain's largest national park is packed much of what is best in British landscape, and yet among it is also that which is unique and could only be the 'Lake District'. To newcomers it can be almost overwhelming, demanding a return again and again to confirm early impressions. Whole libraries of books have been written about the area, whole galleries of pictures have been painted. Perhaps no other part of Britain's countryside has attracted so many ardent devotees. The number of 'Lakers' grows unabated.

Year of designation	1951
Area	880 sq miles (2,280 sq km)
Population	39,835 (1981)
Land use (approx)	
Enclosed farmland	33%
Open country	50%
Commercial forestry	6%
Deciduous woodland	5%
Land ownership (approx)	
National Park	4%
Forestry Commission	5.6%
Water Authority	6.8%
National Trust	24.8%
Natural areas of special interest	
National Nature Reserves	4
Other nature reserves	13
Sites of Special Scientific Interest	79
	(14.2% of park)

Administering authority
Lake District Special Planning Board,
Busher Walk,
Kendal,
Cumbria
LA9 4RH
Tel: (0539) 24555
The whole of the national park is in the county of Cumbria.

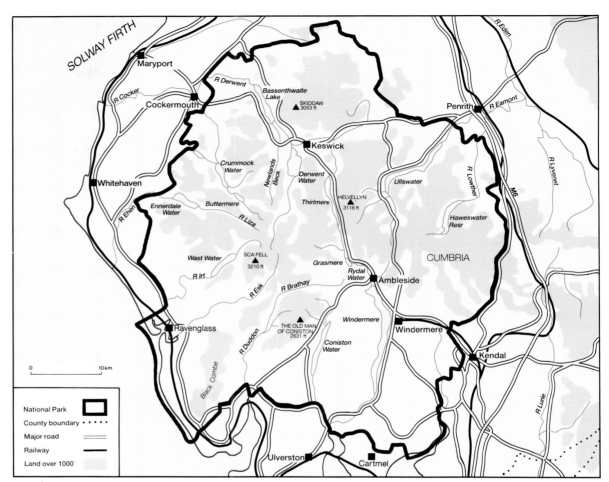

Left:
Lake District National Park, the largest of the parks. Its lakes and mountains have been a source of inspiration to poets and artists for two centuries.

The Lake District can be all things to all men, all of them pleasurable. Beyond the immediate impact of what, if any, can be called a typical Lakeland view: hills, crags, and mountains spilling water, towering over still tarns or lakes rimmed with woodland, and all in happy proportion; there are the lush green dales, and dales within dales, with settlements and villages which look as if they have grown out of their environment. And over the brow of the hills, for the walker, hundreds of square miles of glorious freedom, in a testing, craggy, heaving landscape cleft by hollows and ravines.

Once captured, the Laker finds that the attraction need never wane. For although the shape of the

Lake District National Park.

The Keswick boat landings, Derwent Water.

extreme: the famous Scafell Crag, the Napes on Great Gable, the many in Langdale and Borrowdale. Almost every valley has its climbing crag.

'Mountains are the beginning and the end of all natural scenery'. So said the great John Ruskin, the supreme arbiter of natural landscape. And he spent the last twenty-nine years of his life looking across Coniston Water from his home to the wrinkled east face of Coniston Old Man. The view is a classic, though repeated hundreds of times in the Lake District; a contrast between both ends of the scale: the passive levels of the lake, and behind, the assertive summits sawing the sky, and in between the woodlands, the scatterings of trees and the rock outcrops. A far-off farmstead is dwarfed by the scale. Nothing clashing. A harmony.

Simplified geological map of the Lake District.

Sandstone, shale and limestone

Granite

Skiddaw Slate

Borrowdale Volcanic

Silurian Slate

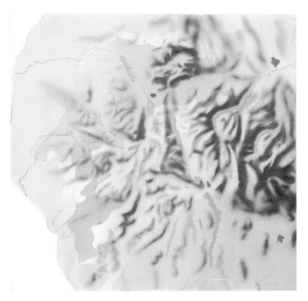

familiar landscapes are unchanging, the moods are ever-varying. Colours modulate not only by seasons, but by hours, with the moving light and shade and cloud patterns, and the stroke of the wind.

Mild-looking crags can suddenly seem to grow and threaten. Silent lakes begin to lap and speak. Brooding trees begin to sway and 'clap their hands'. And that is not all, for the landform is so complicated in fold and fell and field, and curve and crook that it can offer a lifetime of exploration. Even on the busiest bank holiday those who need solitude can find it – often only a little way from the busy bustle.

The opportunities for recreation in the Lake District are abundant. Apart from the vast area of fell land available by let or by right for walkers, there are some 1,860 miles (2,990 km) of public footpaths in the care of the Park Authority, mostly at lower levels, through woods and by lakes and rivers. So not all walkers need to be mountaineers. Of the sixteen lakes, Windermere, Coniston Water, Ullswater and Derwent Water are in effect public highways available for sailing. Several of the other lakes are open for sailing too. Then there are the many rocks for climbing, from the difficult to the

The observant explorer might, however, notice that these mountain scenes fall mainly into three types. If a stroll is taken from the Keswick boat landings to the popular and magnificent viewpoint of Friar's Crag (first to seize Ruskin's attention when he was a boy) one can see two of them. Looking back, the great humped wall of Skiddaw (3,053 ft, 930 m) crowds Keswick, and across the lake one can see the arched and angular outlines of the north-western fells peering over each others' shoulders: very impressive but with few signs of ruggedness.

much neglected height which Wordsworth thought offered one of the best views in England: across to the Isle of Man, and with clarity the hills of Scotland and North Wales.

Turning from Friar's Crag to look *up* Derwent Water one can see those much more aggressive rock formations of the volcanics – the 'Borrowdale Volcanic' series. These very hard rocks formed from lavas and volcanic ash reacted differently through the aeons of erosion. The Ice Ages shattered and broke them up into sharp crags and shoulders. The whole of the central high land beloved by walkers and climbers is in these volcanics: southwards from Derwent Water's east side and up into the head of Borrowdale to the obesity of Great Gable (2,949 ft, 899 m) and the

But on reaching the promontary viewpoint and looking up the lake there is that ever-changing but extraordinary scene – into the jaws of Borrowdale with its jagged, hanging, tree-covered precipitous crags, and if there is good clarity, straight up beyond the high-heaving fells to the highest land in England.

There are two rock types that dominate the scene. Firstly the Skiddaw Slates, the oldest rocks, to the north and north-west. Not the common conception of slate, rather a shale which weathers down into flakes, so that profiles tend to be angular with few crags. Even though the Skiddaw Slates have weathered away over the many thousands of years since the Ice Ages, the fact that they are relatively soft meant that the great earth movements which thrust upwards to build the mountains pushed them higher than other more resistant rocks. The worn remnants of the mountains of the series are none the less impressive. Skiddaw dominates Keswick and Bassenthwaite Lake. Its fiercer-looking neighbour Blencathra (Saddleback) is 2,847 ft (868 m). This whole mass together covers some forty-five square miles. Surrounded by these slates, 4 mile long (6½ km) Bassenthwaite Lake, owned by the Park Authority, is best viewed from the (alas fast and noisy) A66 on its west side. The Skiddaw Slates continue westwards from Derwent Water, from the humps of Cat Bells south-westwards to Buttermere and westwards to Crummock Water, a large area of curves, crests, ridges and valleys worthy of long exploration. Westwards again the slates dip below the sea, but there is one more exposure in the park – in the south-west at Black Combe (1,970 ft, 600 m), a

Blencathra, a Skiddaw Slate landscape from Castlerigg stone circle.

Wast Water, with Great Gable centre background and the slopes of Lingmell and the Scafells to its right.

sprawl of the Scafells with Scafell Pike, the highest point in England (3,210 ft, 978 m); all of the land from the west by the head of Ennerdale Water through Coniston Old Man, Bowfell (2,960 ft, 902 m), the distinctive Langdale Pikes and Grasmere fells; Helvellyn (3,118 ft, 949 m) and its long range; and Fairfield and the High Street range.

It is the variety of rock types around the lakes which gives each its unique character. Derwent Water is a superb mixture of contrasts with a hundred viewpoints, high and low, around it. Buttermere's beautiful little lake has the severe slopes of the Skiddaw Slates on its north-east side, and on its other side the impact of the crags and deep combes of High Crag and High Stile. Its longer neighbour only a mile further down the valley, Crummock Water, is more open, and mellows as it widens into the softer slates of the lovely vale of Lorton. Ennerdale has its head in the towering volcanics of Pillar and Steeple and Gable. Its lake laps granite but melts completely into its wider foot in the slates. Wast Water is all drama, with those sensational screes from Illgill Head plunging down its side, and even further down to its dark depths of 250 ft (76 m). And at its head that glorious prospect of mountains dominated by Kirk Fell, Great Gable, and the shoulder of the Scafells. From this the National Park took its emblem. East of Helvellyn the 7 mile length (11 km) of Ullswater curves from its head, enclosed in the high-reaching fells, and in its

Striding Edge, Helvellyn, in winter. An arrêt between two coves.

lower reaches turns and leaves them all behind to enter a muted landscape of the Skiddaw Slates.

The favourite little lakes of Rydal Water and Grasmere in the Wordsworth country are near the edge of the volcanics. Though the heights are modest, their sides, shaggy with trees, still make their presence felt.

If one climbs Todd Crag, on the low volcanic height of Loughrigg, by Ambleside, there is revealed a beautiful view southwards over a different landscape again: the third type of mountain scene. Windermere grabs the attention at once. Impressive enough, though one can see only a portion of its $10\frac{1}{2}$ mile (18 km) length. But hereabout the hills are more restrained, undulating, largely tree covered. This more recent rock southwards is

the solidified mud and silts of the sedimentary Silurian, which once covered most of the area but was largely swept away by the Ice Age glaciers. The ice in fact pushed down from the central heights with such force that it gouged deep into this softer rock to make the lake, deepening its bed to 200 ft (60 m), and below sea level.

The main area of Silurian rocks in the park lies between Windermere and Coniston Water. The soil is acid and gives sufficient depth to support forest; there is that wonderful sweep of hardwoods above Windermere to Claife Heights (National Trust), and Grizedale Forest's conifers to the south-west. At Coniston Water again it is the contrasts that give the great attraction to the 5 mile (8 km) long lake. This time bounded by the woods and hills of the Silurian on the east, but to the west is that great wall of the Coniston Old Man range. In the southern part of the Silurian are the lovely old woodlands, including those at Rusland, above Backbarrow, and those at the south-western end of Windermere, in the care and ownership of the Park Authority.

Two other rock types need mention. To the south-east there are two Carboniferous Limestone 'scars' (ridges). Scout Scar by the park boundary near

Glenridding, Ullswater. A typical U-shaped glaciated valley on the east side of Helvellyn.

After the Ice Age and thousands of years of storm erosion, about 10,000 years ago the botanical advance was able to begin, first with alpine and tundra vegetation, then later with birch and pine, willow and alder. Finally came the extensive woodlands, predominantly oak, to a height of around 2,500 ft (760 m). The animals thrived too, and on their heels came the human population.

The first evidence of human settlement dates from the Neolithic period. From around 4,000 years ago the Lake District had its first major industry: the making of stone axes. Several axe 'factories' have been discovered since the first site was indentified in Langdale in 1947. There are specimens of the 'Langdale' axes in many museums of Britain for the industry enjoyed a country-wide trade. The axes were made from an extremely hard 'tuff', a vein of rock which runs below the central peaks. The axe, polished and sharpened with sand on the coast, was an efficient instrument. I have felled a birch tree with one with little difficulty. It was the cutting down and burning of the forest which began to change the face of the Lake District.

In the late Neolithic/Early Bronze Age period several stone circles were built in the area,

Swinside stone circle, by Black Combe in the west of the national park.

Kendal gives a superb view from its high cliff over the Silurian landscape to the central volcanics. Whitbarrow Scar to its south-west is largely a nature reserve. There are also the granite outcrops at Ennerdale, Wasdale and Eskdale; and in the east at Shap, where granite was quarried for some London buildings including St Pancras station and the Albert Memorial.

Prominent landscape features were shaped by the Ice Age. At one time the whole of the Lake District, apart from the highest peaks, was covered by ice. As the glaciers eventually ground their way through the valleys to gouge out the lakes, they also deepened and plucked away at the side walls and left higher valleys 'hanging'. The glaciated pattern can be seen throughout the valleys radiating from the higher hub of the central peaks: lakes, waterfalls cascading from high valleys, water cupped in tarns high on the north and east facing fells, 'coves' where the ice lingered longest. In places the coves almost meet to produce 'arrêts' (causeways) in between. The best known are Striding Edge on Helvellyn, the most popular and exciting ascent path, its neighbour Swirral Edge, and Sharp Edge on Blencathra.

Great Gable from the Scafells. The cloud level is about the height of the maximum ice covering. Only the Lake District's highest peaks were uncovered.

traditionally called 'druid circles', but predating the advent of the Celtic priests by centuries. The two most notable are at Castlerigg near Keswick, in a remarkably dramatic scene circled by mountains, and Swinside stone circle on farm land on a spur of Black Combe, which is also in an evocative if different setting. Keats wrote of a visit to Castlerigg on a dull day in *Hyperian*:

'– a dismal cirque
Of Druid stones, upon a forlorn moor,
When the chill rain begins at shut of eve
In dull November, and their chancel vault,
The heaven itself, is blinded throughout night.'

Over 800 ft (240 m) above Eskdale on a shelf in the mountain side is astonishing evidence of the Roman occupation. In this unlikely place the ruins of Hardknott Fort, *Mediobogdum*, are a sight to rouse the imagination. The views from it are sublime: across Eskdale to the highest land in England, and westwards to the sea. To build it here the cohort of 'Dalmatians' (from modern-day Yugoslavia) had to construct a road through rock and over the high wild passes of Wrynose and Hardknott, in country

Aira Force, by Ullswater. Owned by the National Trust it is one of the more spectacular of many waterfalls.

Plan of Castlerigg stone circle.

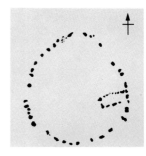

Part of Castlerigg stone circle near Keswick.

Castle') can be seen. Part of the walls stand to their original height.

After a stay of three centuries the Roman armies withdrew and the Romano-British were left to work out their own destiny. From the seventh century Anglian settlers spread their influence throughout Britain and the native Celts were forced into the moors of the south-west, into Wales, and into Scotland of which at that time the Lake District, in the north-west corner of England, was a part. The British of Wales and this north-west part of England called themselves 'the compatriots' or in Celtic, the 'Cymri'; hence later 'Cumberland', and from 1974 the old name 'Cumbria'.

There is evidence however that the Angles favoured the fertile coastal plain. In Irton churchyard in the west of the park is a remarkable thousand year old Anglian cross, standing 10 ft (3½ m) high and covered in carved decoration. But just over two miles north of this cross is another even more remarkable one. This stands 13 ft (4 m) high in Gosforth churchyard and is of a slightly later period. It is pure Viking; the Christian story of the triumph of good over evil on one side, and Norse mythology on the other sides. The proximity of the

perfect for guerilla warfare! Much of the fort's walls remain. The ruin of the bath house can be seen below the fort, and up above a parade ground was constructed – the only level land in that billowing mass of rock and crag.

The first Roman advance into the Lake District came after AD 79 when Gnaeus Julius Agricola came north to settle accounts with the devious Brigante tribe. The northbound road from Chester came through Kendal to Penrith, and an untraceable branch led off to Waterhead, Ambleside, where a fort was built close to Windermere's shore. This was *Galava*. Only the foundations can now be seen. From here one unrevealed route went north-east, and eventually surprisingly high along the 2,500 foot (762 m) ridge of the High Street range, probably improving a British road built above the bogs and forest of the valleys. The route westwards from Waterhead fort to Wrynose cannot at first be traced, but sections over the passes can be seen. From Hardknott Fort the road went down Eskdale to the Roman port at Ravenglass. The fort here has been destroyed by sea encroachment and the construction of the railway, but remarkably the impressive bath house ruin (locally called 'Walls

The north-west gateway of Hardknott Roman fort. The Scafells in the distance.

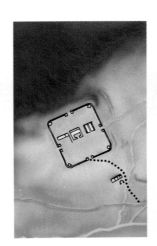

Plan of Mediobogdum.

The ninth-century Anglian cross at Irton.

Fourteenth century 'pele tower' at Kentmere Hall.

two crosses suggests that both settlers lived peacefully together, for by this time the Vikings did not come as sea-raiders. The two races did not compete for the same land. The Angles wanted flatter lands for their ox ploughs, the Vikings the higher land for pasturage.

That the settlement of Norwegian Vikings from Ireland, Isle of Man, and the west coast of Scotland

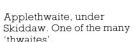

Applethwaite, under Skiddaw. One of the many 'thwaites'.

was extensive is evident in the very many place names. For instance, the place names ending in 'thwaite'. Thwaite is Norse/Irish for clearing. The mountains here are fells from 'fjall'; the valleys are dales from 'dalr'. Streams are all becks from 'bekkr'. Small lakes are tarns from 'tjörn'. Waterfalls are forces from 'foss'. There are very many more examples.

After the Dark Ages and the Norman invasion William Rufus took the area from Scotland in the late eleventh century and castles were built to enforce the Norman law. The best examples are outside the park at Penrith, Brougham, Cockermouth and Egremont. However, for centuries the border was changeable and troublesome and this had a lasting effect on the area's economy. To protect family and breeding stock from the border raiders wealthier landowners built defensive towers: 'pele towers'. There are a number of examples in the park, some were later incorporated into stately homes.

The greatest economic influence in the medieval period came from the monasteries (occasionally severely troubled by border raiders). Furness Abbey, outside the park near Dalton, with a daughter abbey at Calder, became a wealthy major

Brougham Castle near Penrith. Dating from the twelfth century.

The ruins of Calder Abbey in the west of the national park. Calder was a daughter abbey of Furness. It was twice sacked by the Scots and twice restored.

Wall End Farm in Langdale. Cared for by the National Trust it is basically of seventeenth and eighteenth century construction.

employer, founding the wool, woodland and mining industries. The abbeys' Dissolution must have drastically disrupted the economy for some time.

The seventeenth century brought some long-needed stability to the border when James I unified Scotland and England. It seemed that the threat from raiders was over. Tenant farmers were given security too by a King's Bench decision in 1625 which recognised the service given by their forefathers in the border wars. The economy was healthy and the time of building began. Farm houses and barns, previously of wood, were now rebuilt with stone, and there are many examples of this period surviving today. Drystone walls were also built, although the majority of the walls which stride over the fells, often looking like a great net, were built as a result of the Enclosure Acts between 1760 and 1850. The amount of human heavy labour in their making defies calculation.

Before the second half of the eighteenth century roads were poor. The larger lakes were used as important highways, a practice that continued into this century. The common way into the Lake District from the south for the first visitors, before the development of turnpike roads, was across the sands of Morecambe Bay where there are quicksands, deep river channels, and the tide rushes in quicker than a man can run. From medieval times a monk would guide the low-tide crossings. This later became the responsibility of the Duchy of Lancaster. A guide is still appointed and the road across the sands is still shown on Ordnance Survey maps as a highway; and so it is.

From the middle of the eighteenth century a new interest in natural landscape, encouraged by the popularity of the landscape artists of Europe, particularly the Roman school and especially works by Claude Lorraine, led to the 'discovery' of the Lake District and the production of better maps and guide books, the first best-seller by a local Jesuit priest, Father West. Among the earlier visiting artists were JMW Turner, who came a number of times, John Constable and Gainsborough. But artists who came to stay made a reasonable living. These included William Green and William Westall, praised by Wordsworth, Sir George Beaumont, John Harden, and JC Ibbetson.

One of the earliest writer visitors was Thomas Gray in 1769. His glowing account of his visit encouraged more interest. Wordsworth and his

Among the many other writers who came to the Lakes was Lamb, who visited his friend Coleridge in 1802. Thomas de Quincey married a local girl (to the Wordsworth's disapproval) and rented Dove Cottage when the Wordsworths left. Here he wrote his *Confessions of an Opium Eater*. John Keats was an enthusiastic 'Laker'. Shelley stayed in Keswick with his new bride for several months. Sir Walter Scott was a visitor to the Wordsworths on several

Room at Rydal Mount with William and Mary Wordsworth. Part of an engraving by William Westall.

talented sister Dorothy put the final seal of approval on the district when they moved into a rented Grasmere cottage in December 1799, and in the next eight years William wrote some of the greatest poetry in the English language, including *'Prelude'*, *Intimations of Immortality*, *Lyrical Ballads* and much else. He brought his bride Mary Hutchinson to the cottage in 1802, and when the family expanded they had to move to larger quarters in Grasmere and later to Rydal Mount. 'Dove Cottage' is now open to the public and visited by thousands of devotees every year, from all over the world.

Wordsworth's great friend and inspirational collaborator, Coleridge, moved to the Lakes in 1800, renting Greta Hall in Keswick (now part of a school). Coleridge's brother-in-law Southey went on a visit to the house and stayed for the rest of his life, some forty years. The health of Coleridge and his mental state deteriorated rapidly from his addiction to laudanum and he left the area in 1804. Southey, a prolific writer, became poet laureate in 1813. He died in 1843 and his memorial in Crosthwaite church at Keswick was written by his friend Wordsworth, who took his place as poet laureate.

Kirkstone Pass, the highest road in the national park. From the second half of the eighteenth century roads were improved and tourism became easier.

The cottage at Town End, Grasmere later called 'Dove Cottage'. The home of the Wordsworths when William was at the height of his powers.

occasions. His *Guy Mannering* and *Redgauntlet* have Cumbrian settings. Harriet Martineau took residence in Ambleside in 1845. Her visitors included Charlotte Brontë, John Bright, Ralph Waldo Emerson, Mathew Arnold, and Mary Ann Evans (George Eliot).

John Ruskin settled at Brantwood on the east side of Coniston Water in 1871 and lived there, well respected by the local people, until his death in 1900. James Spedding welcomed to his home, at Mirehouse by Bassenthwaite Lake, his friends Thomas Carlyle, Edward Fitzgerald and Alfred Lord Tennyson. Much of the inspiration for *Idylls of the King* came from Tennyson's Lake District visits. Brantwood and Mirehouse are now open to the public.

These are names familiar to every British schoolchild, but how many know that Seathwaite in Borrowdale in the Lake District is the wettest place in England? It has 131 in annually, although the heights above might take 150 to 180 in. However, the amount of rainfall is surprisingly less away from the central heights. Keswick has 57 in, Penrith 35 in. Although the head of Langdale might get 170 in, twelve miles away at Windermere it is 60 in. As the dominant Atlantic airstream is influenced by the mild Gulf Stream, winter snow-fall is seldom great. The district will never be a ski resort.

Woodland which once covered the mountains has gone owing to the action of man. Centuries of grazing sheep have prevented its regeneration, and the high grasslands have deteriorated to a point where nardus (mat grass) covers great areas. It is unpalatable even to the local 'Herdwick' breed of sheep, as is bracken which has spread everywhere in the past fifty years. The thin acid soils of the fells restrict botanical interest to the gills (ravines) and wet flushes, where minerals well to the surface. It is here that the alpines are found. Ravens and peregrine falcons rule the fells and crags, but golden eagles have made a welcome return to the Lake District and one pair has bred successfully for some years.

Now ten per cent of the whole park is tree covered, but only half of this is native broadleaved, the rest being alien conifer forest. Luckily 5,000 acres (2,024 ha) of deciduous woodland is safe in the hands of the National Trust. The Park Authority has more than a thousand acres (400 ha) and has a policy of grant-aiding small woodland schemes throughout the park. Some of the woods are Sites of Special

The east shore of Coniston Water. Part of the Old Man range in the background.

Scientific Interest because of their abundance of mosses, liverworts and lichens.

The animals of Lakeland woods include the abundant roe deer, a lovely animal normally only seen at dawn and dusk. There are red squirrel populations in many woods. The red has not been ousted by the alien grey squirrel, which so far has not succeeded in invading the district.

Mallard, tufted duck, teal, merganser, goosander and mute swans breed among the lakes and in winter they are joined by goldeneye, pochard, widgeon, shovellers and cormorants. Whooper swans are welcome visitors too, and with good luck one can sometimes spot the great northern, red throated and black throated divers. Greylags and Canada geese graze the shoreline grasses. Trout are common in the lakes. Char, a kind of deep-water trout, is found in Windermere, Wast Water and Ennerdale Water. Ullswater contains a rare fish, the schelly, sometimes referred to as 'freshwater herring', but not related. The vendace, another rare fish, *is* related to the schelly, and is found only in Derwent Water and Bassenthwaite Lake.

The problems facing the national park have much to do with its tremendous popularity. Access via the

Golden eagle.

A young red squirrel.

133

A roebuck in summer. Like the red deer it sheds its antlers in the winter, and re-grows them.

The round-the-lake boat service on Derwent Water which links up with several delightful low-level footpaths.

M6 is so easy that regular visitors are taken from a huge area. It is possible to meet walkers on Helvellyn who have journeyed from London for the weekend. Several hundreds of miles of the fell footpath network in the care of the Park, and also the National Trust on their land, are badly eroded by the boots of well over a million walkers each year. Several millions more walkers use the low-level paths in the valleys and around the lakes. The Park Authority has to see that all the routes are usable, that they are signed from the road side, and that stiles and gates are maintained. Normally the responsibility for stiles and gates rests with the landowner, but where wear and tear is obviously caused by visitors the Park Authority shoulders the task. For all this work the Park employs teams of workmen and rangers, and has the support of many volunteers, particularly those provided by the British Trust for Conservation Volunteers.

Hill farming is still a major employer in the Lakes even though current economics has led to the loss of many jobs and a decrease of well over a quarter of the farms. The problem, social as well as economic, is not solved by the increase in tourist related employment. Farmers in the Lake District show extraordinary tolerance to the disruptive pressures of tourism. To ease their problems from this cause, and to conserve the farming landscape which might otherwise deteriorate from lack of manpower, the Park Authority started an 'upland management' scheme with the support of the Countryside Commission in 1969. It has been much expanded since and the farming community accepts the assistance gratefully. Following the success of the scheme similar initiatives have been taken up by other national park authorities.

Incidents calling on the services of the efficient voluntary mountain rescue teams hover around 200 annually. This is more than any other part of Britain, which is indicative of the huge number of hill walkers. Apart from supporting the rescue services with grants and ranger manpower, it is part of the duty of the Park's ranger and information services to promote mountain safety. One aid is the 'phone-in' weather forecast service which was pioneered by the Park with the support of the tourist authority (Windermere 5151).

The Park operates an anti-litter service which removes litter by the ton annually. It is aided by the efforts of hundreds of volunteers, particularly from

the Park's voluntary warden service. A sad reflection on the habits of an untidy minority of visitors.

The Park Authority operates information and visitor centres in the main tourist areas, and information in the field is offered by the ranger and voluntary warden services. The Park has the first and the largest Visitor Centre at Brockhole on the shores of Windermere. Here, with the aid of displays, lectures and special events visitors can be helped to see and appreciate all that the superb variety of the Lake District's landscape can offer.

The success of the Park Authority in its planning policy is in what is *not* seen. In spite of commercial pressures and the heavy demand for new house building there is no ugly development to spoil the Lake District's unique and beautiful blend of hill and rock, dales and settlements, lakes and moving water. As a national park the 'District of the Lakes in the North of England' will continue to offer solace and inspiration to everyone who, in Wordsworth's words:

'has an eye to perceive, and a heart to enjoy.'

Coniston Water shore at Old Brown Howe in winter, a National Park owned picnic area.

Although the Park does not acquire land as a matter of policy, opportunity purchases of important sites have been made to secure public access and protect the landscape. Crown land made over to the Authority includes the Blawith and Torver commons by Coniston, and Caldbeck commons behind Skiddaw.

Northumberland National Park

Northumberland National Park is the most northerly of the parks. It is no longer a frontier, but, on the remains of the Roman Wall or with only the wind for company among the wild folded fells, time seems to have taken on a different meaning. All now is utter peace. It is the peace of an old abandoned battlefield. The lonely hills and the broken wall are now silent witnesses to a long history of violence and lawlessness. In the south of the park was drawn the northern boundary of the great Roman Empire. To the north was the line between those who claimed to be Scots or English; and sometimes if there was profit in it, changed from one nationality to another. Here was the Middle March of the border law where robber horsemen rode by

Year of designation	1956
Area	398 sq miles (1,031 sq km)
Population	2,219 (1981)
Land use (approx)	
Enclosed farmland	9.5%
Open country	71.0%
Commercial forestry	19.0%
Deciduous woodland	0.59%
Land ownership (approx)	
National Park	0.2%
Forestry Commission	18.9%
Water Authority	1.2%
National Trust	0.7%
Ministry of Defence	22.6%
Natural areas of special interest	
National Nature Reserves	2
Other nature reserves	20
Sites of Special Scientific Interest	20

Administering authority
Northumberland National Park &
Countryside Department,
(Northumberland County Council)
Eastburn,
South Park,
Hexham,
Northumberland,
NE46 1BS
Tel: (0434) 605555
The national park is wholly within the county of Northumberland.

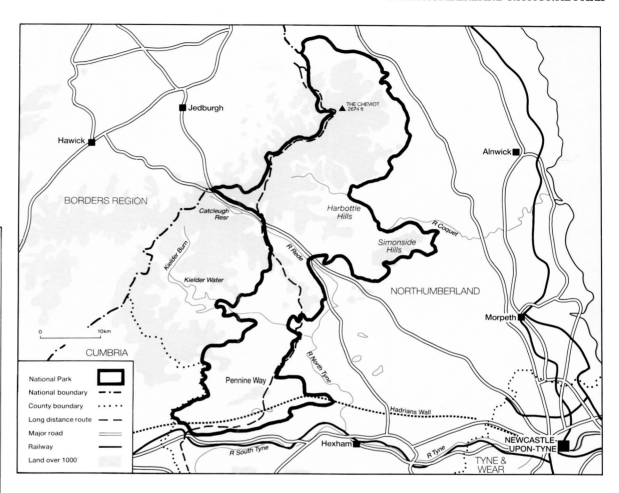

Left:
Northumberland National Park. The most remote of the parks; here was the northern frontier of the Roman Empire.

moonlight. Here clan feuds were manipulated by ruthless politicians, and beacons called the people to arms.

North of the escarpments of Hadrian's Wall across the rising land of forest, moor, heather and grassland to the high green mass of the distant hills nothing seems to have changed for centuries. It is a man-made landscape, yet sparsely populated. It is the least visited of the national parks, and even then the visitor pressure is mainly confined to the Roman Wall and the sixty-six miles of the Pennine Way. For those who savour remoteness, there are vast acres of it. For the naturalist there is a variety of unusual habitats, some of international importance. For

Northumberland National Park.

137

the Ice Ages and the subsequent flow of melt water hollowed out the valleys and depressions and deposited boulder clay on the lee side of the hills, while boulders of Cheviot volcanics were carried by the ice far to the south.

When the climate improved 10,000 years ago, vegetation became established in waves as conditions favoured one range of species or another. Wet periods led to the formation of peat beds.

As elsewhere, the first settlers to leave their mark here were the energetic Neolithic agriculturalists who cleared the forest with fire and stone axes.

Windyhaugh, looking towards the Border Ridge.

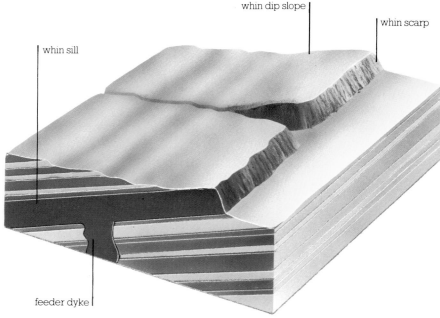

those who want to reach back to the beginning of time what can be seen can surely fire the imagination.

Yet the peaceful landscape of this region began in violence. The Cheviot Hills were volcanoes early in the Devonian period about 400 million years ago, showering the area with ash and dust and then covering it with larva flows. When these cooled and solidified more magma found its way upwards but cooled under the earth's crust to form granite. Subsequently, over aeons, climatic conditions eroded the lavas away to expose the granite now seen around the Cheviots. Then, for sixty million years, the area around the Cheviots was covered by seas of fluctuating levels which left sediments that later became sandstones, shales and limestones.

At the end of this period earth movements affected the Cheviots area and magma found its way upwards into weaknesses in the rock beds above. In one extensive area it found lateral weakness – in between the rock layers – and spread out under the surface to produce, after the erosion of later times, a major geological feature from Greenhead, in the south west of the park, to the Northumberland coast at Bamburgh: the Great Whin Sill. Glacial flows of

Thyme. The flora species of the park are generally restricted to those which grow in acidic or impoverished soils. Exceptions occur on the dip slope of the Whin Sill where the soil is enriched by quartz-dolerite. Thyme, rockrose, cranesbill and wild chive are some of the species found here.

'Langdale' axes from the Lake District have been found here, proving that the inhabitants were advanced enough to open communications and trade. They buried their dead under long cairns, remains of which can be found in the park. Again, inroads into the forests were continued when the population was increased by the settlers of the Bronze Age. They were a religious people. Stone circles and henges in the north of Britain often date from the early part of this period but there are no stone 'cathedrals' here like Stonehenge, or even

Diagram showing how the Whin Sill was formed. Magma was squeezed laterally between rock layers. The 'scarp' is roughly to the north, the 'dip' south.

governor and strategist Julius Agricola to consolidate Roman rule after AD 78, following his successful campaign against the Welsh in Snowdonia. The Roman method of conquest was to penetrate the area with good roads, placing forts at strategic points to defend them. From bases at Chester and York, roads were made to Carlisle in the west and Corbridge in the east. Between Corbridge and Carlisle a road was made through the Tyne-Irthing gap, probably an 'improvement' of an existing British road. This road, the 'Stanegate', can still be followed westwards through the park between Grindon Hill in the south to where it leaves the park at Greenhead.

'Cup and ring' marks on fell sandstone, Lordenshaws near Rothbury. The strange markings must have had religious significance. They are common in Ireland, and also occur in Spain and Portugal. They are present on stones in the Pennines and north of England, and southern Scotland, but plentiful in Northumberland.

Castlerigg in the Lake District. Maybe the remnants here are 'chapels'? Five stones of a larger circle remain standing by the Cheviots at Threestoneburn to the west of South Middleton, and four stones stand in the remains of a circle at Goatstones, ten miles north of Hexham. On the top of one of these are carved some thirteen 'cup and ring' marks, typical of the period.

The dead were often buried in stone-lined chambers covered with round cairns, and many of these have been found in the park. But only the trained eye of the archaeologist can find the settlement sites, for the huts would have been made of wood and thatch which left little trace. Stone piles reveal field clearances. These farmers probably lived in relative peace.

An inflow of Iron Age people with a common language and culture brought a growth in population, a tribal system, and a fondness for war. The Romans had fought the 'Celts' in Europe and between AD 43 and 50 they had invaded and conquered them in the south of England. In a northern campaign ending in AD 74 the disciplined legions of governor Petillius Cerialis successfully overcame resistance. But it was left to the brilliant

The 'Mare and Foal', ancient standing stones near Shield on the Wall.

Stanegate was defended by several forts. One was at *Vindolanda* on the park's southern boundary. This can be seen by turning off the B6318 at the National Park's information centre at Once Brewed. (A visit here is essential.) A narrow road leads to the Stanegate and the *Vindolanda* site where there is much to see. This fort was later less useful as new forts were built on the Wall, but a thriving village developed here and its remains, managed by the Vindolanda Trust, are revealing. Fascinating finds are displayed in the museum, but the essential and

The Wall may have already been started when Hadrian came north in the early 120s. He appointed Aulus Platorius Nepos as governor and the massive eight-year building programme began between Newcastle and the Solway, at least eighty Roman miles – 73½ miles (118 km). The builders were craftsmen of the 2nd, 6th and 20th legions. The whole section from the east to the River Irthing was built of stone, and beyond, westwards into today's Cumbria, with wide ramparts of turf. A deep ditch or 'vallum' was dug which effectively delineated the military area of the Wall, and ditches were dug in front.

The Wall was about 15 ft (4½ m) high topped by a 6 ft (2 m) parapet. At every Roman mile there was a substantial fortlet, or 'milecastle', with two turrets between each. The milecastles could house some fifty men on two floors. They were provided with doorways, or 'sally ports', for the Roman tactics did not envisage a static defence. At an alarm the men were to rush out with the aim of trapping the invaders against the Wall or ditch. It was decided to build new forts directly on the Wall, abandoning some on the Stanegate. Sixteen were built, thus sealing the frontier. The garrison of the Wall could

Replicas of Hadrian's Wall at *Vindolanda*.

exciting exhibit is the replica of a section of the Roman Wall.

The fort at the crossroads at Corbridge, *Corstopitum*, was also a supply base. The remains to be seen now are a part of the military town which once covered some 40 acres (16 ha). A museum displays objects found during excavation of the fort.

From Corbridge the road from York continued northwards into Scotland. This was Dere Street, now for much of its length outside the park under the A68, but it deviates to continue in the park from Blakehope across Redesdale and through remote countryside in the Cheviot Hills.

Following Agricola's triumphs in Scotland to gain a strong position on the Forth-Clyde line, he was recalled to Rome in AD 84. Scotland was abandoned in AD 100 after the Roman legions in Britain suffered a cut-back, and the northern frontier became the Stanegate. Under the Emperor Trajan the Roman positions in many places were strengthened south of the Stanegate, but something had to be done eventually to make a more secure line: a wall was an obvious choice since nature provided natural ramparts and northern escarpments – the Great Whin Sill.

The Stanegate as it runs through the Roman town of *Corstopitum* near Corbridge.

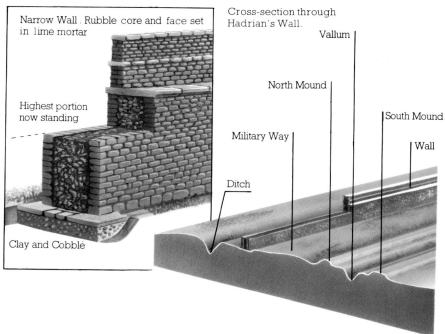

Narrow Wall. Rubble core and face set in lime mortar

Highest portion now standing

Clay and Cobble

Cross-section through Hadrian's Wall.

Vallum

North Mound

South Mound

Military Way

Wall

Ditch

Diagrammatic cross section showing the main components of Hadrian's frontier: vallum wall and ditch.

be held by about 10,000 men, supported by reinforcements rushed up Dere Street from York if necessary.

Where the Wall crossed the North Tyne River north west of Hexham there was the fort of *Cilurnum* (Chesters). It defended the bridge, the abutments of which can still be seen. The buildings here were quite substantial and the bath house between the fort and the river was surprisingly large. The next fort westwards on the Wall was *Brocolitia*. The site can be seen after a bend on the road which follows the Wall. (There is a car park on the left.) The only remains are grass-covered ramparts, but the main attraction here is south of the site where a temple of Mithras was excavated in 1949. The findings were removed to the Museum of Archaeology at Newcastle, but a replica has been placed in position. To some it might have a strangely fascinating atmosphere. Some people may even find it eerie.

West again was the largest fort on this section of the Wall, at Housesteads. This was *Vercovicium*. There is much to see here: the bases of gateways, ramparts, the all-important granaries, headquarters buildings, barracks and outside a civil settlement.

Hadrian's Wall remains. The view east from Walltown.

There is a museum and information centre on the site. Walking north east by the Wall one must go to the high point at Sewingshields Crag, and imagine oneself as a Roman soldier from Spain or Africa looking across at the airy view to the barbarians' northern territory. In a cave somewhere here, it was said, lives King Arthur and his men awaiting the trumpet call to summon them to Britain's aid. (Nonsense, the Welsh will argue, the cave is in Snowdonia.) A walk westwards from Housesteads on the Wall brings one to another great viewpoint on Holbank Crags.

West again from Housesteads, the Wall reaches its highest point at 1,132 ft (345 m) to the west of Steel Rigg which is reached by a right turn down a minor road by Twice Brewed Inn. A walk can be made to the height west of the car park, but a walk on the Wall eastwards, too, is recommended for a viewpoint over the little lake of Crag Lough.

Westwards from here was Great Chesters fort, *Aesica.* (Turn right at Milecastle Inn.) There is little left beyond grass-covered ramparts and foundations of the barracks and guard room, but there are good milecastle remains to the east. Just before reaching the park's western boundary at

The north gate of the Housesteads Roman fort. The wall leads off to Sewingshields Crag in the background.

The wall at Cuddy's Crag, west of Housesteads.

Greenhead is the fort of *Carvoran*. Here again there is little remaining but there is a Museum of the Roman Army. A few miles beyond the park boundary, the Wall crossed the River Irthing near Birdoswald and was guarded by *Camboglanna*. This is currently (1988) being excavated. The view down from the site's shelf over the Irthing valley is classic.

Hadrian's successor was Antoninus Pius. In AD 138, for reasons unknown, he chose to abandon the Wall and to push the frontier up to the Forth-Clyde line where he constructed a wall of turf, the Antonine Wall. But towards the end of the century the frontier fell back to Hadrian's Wall. In the next century the Wall was twice abandoned and over-run as the governors Albinus and Allectus in turn withdrew the garrison to Europe in unsuccessful bids for personal power. At the beginning of the fourth century the Wall was secure, but then at last in 367 there was a concerted attack by Picts, Scots and Saxons, helped by the treachery, it was said, of some of the auxiliaries who changed sides for a share of the loot. Count Theodosius was sent with reinforcements by Emperor Valentinian to deal with the problem. He retook the Wall and caused repairs and renovations but things were never to be the same again. The defence elsewhere against increasing numbers of coastal raids was a drain on resources and morale. Rome, too, was cursed by political troubles and threatened by enemies. When troops were withdrawn from Britain for the defence of Rome, it was the beginning of the end of the Wall. By this time the forts were fortified villages – the civilians having abandoned the vulnerable settlements. An appeal then by the Romana/British inhabitants to the Emperor Honorius for support received the dry reply that they should have to see to their own defence.

The last use of the Wall was very much later and sadly destructive. When Charles Stuart advanced so easily through Carlisle with his Highlanders in the 1745 rebellion one excuse was that there was no good road from Newcastle for the swift movement of troops and artillery. The Stanegate was inadequate. After the defeat of the Jacobites it was thought that a new road was necessary to prevent further similar troubles. In 1751 General Wade began to build a new road, and for much of its length he chose a route close to, or on the Wall, using its masonry as a base. This is now largely the B6318. Where the road deviates from it, the Wall is better preserved. This includes a substantial stretch between

Sewingshields and Greenhead in the national park. However, even here much of the masonry has been 'quarried' for building.

I do not know when I have best enjoyed walking along the Wall. In curlew-crying early summer with the flowers of the Whin Sill in bloom? Or once in the winter with a sudden storm from the furious north raking the ramparts with hailstones? But a walk on the Wall is always rewarding; everyone does it. Its popularity causes wear and tear problems and the Park Authority and others with responsibilities along its length have had to work out a conservation strategy for its secure future. Plans are also being made to create a long distance footpath along the Wall, but it may be a few years before this is ready for holiday walkers.

Signs of the sites and buildings of the remaining centuries are scarce. The 'palace' of King Edwin of Northumbria (seventh century) was discovered in the 1950s near the park boundary under the hill, Yeavering Bell. Paulinus, the Christian missionary who baptised the converted king, is said by Bede to have baptised many others here in the River Glen. The site of one of the battles of the rival Saxon kings, when King Oswald defeated Cadwallon in 634, is

Black Middens bastle in North Tynedale. Bastle houses were built by wealthier farmers in the sixteenth century as defence against raiders. On alarm stock would be barred in at the ground floor. The upper floor would be occupied by the family. A wooden ladder (replaced later by steps) would be drawn up behind them.

marked by a cross by the wall and military road east of Brunton.

That there are few buildings in the region has much to do with restricted areas of good arable land. It also has a lot to do with the troubles which brought lawlessness and chaos for centuries. The border wars brought problems enough. The pony-riding reivers have been romanticised in the border ballads, but to the feuding families which occupied the area in density, cattle stealing and what we now call 'the protection racket' was a way of life. They contributed a new word to the English language – 'black mail' (black rent). The law officers, the Wardens of the Marches, had a formidable task (though sometimes the reivers could be politically useful). Tynedale and Redesdale on the English side of the border were generally considered to be hotbeds of crime. One instance was recorded by the Bishop of Durham who said, after the reivers of Tynedale had fought at Flodden, that they not only robbed the vanquished Scots, but also took the opportunity to make off with baggage and horses from the English camp!

After the union of the crowns, James I determined to put an end to centuries of border trouble on both sides. There were mass hangings. A hundred 'outlaws' from Tynedale and Redesdale were 'enlisted for service in Ireland'.

Gradually into the following century a more settled atmosphere encouraged some building in stone. The larger landowners then considered it safe to invest in their land, using money made elsewhere. Land had a price at last and some changed hands. Farming methods improved and wet areas were drained. New roads were made. Common lands were enclosed by stone walls and hedges, and lime was used for the first time to sweeten the pastures. It gradually became a farming revolution. This did not necessarily do much for the tenant farmers, many of whom were dispossessed in the reorganisation and had to seek a living in the growing industries of Tyneside. The population of the countryside greatly declined. Some of the freeholders were forced to sell out and those who stayed could not necessarily afford the farm improvement methods of the larger landowners and were sometimes worse off than the remaining tenants. Although nowadays there is no poverty, to an extent the same situation applies today. The small farmer in the southern part of the park struggles to keep his farm viable. The varied enterprises of

The merlin ranges the hills where curlew, snipe and golden plover breed.

Mid-winter in the Cheviot Hills. The view from Windy Gyle on the Pennine Way.

larger estates affords them some stability.

So the generally deserted landscape of the park largely reflects the changes that reached a climax two and a half centuries ago. Changes may continue to occur but, in common with all national parks, the Park Authority must have a concern for the welfare of the small farmers and assist them with an upland management service and any other means possible.

Enclosed farming land accounts for only 9.5 per cent of the park area, by far the smallest proportion of all the national parks. Seventy per cent of the land is open country – a greater area in comparison with the other national parks. But over a fifth of the whole land, between the Rede and the Coquet, is owned by the Ministry of Defence, established here before the park's designation. There are usable public rights of way to the north of this area, outside the firing ranges. The Ministry of Defence is, however, not without sympathy for the cause of conservation. With the Park's consent, they acquired a 1,050 acre (425 ha) conifer plantation and are converting it into a mixed broadleaved coniferous forest.

About another fifth of the park is in the ownership of the Forestry Commission and the public are encouraged to use their marked drives and paths. There is an agreement with the National Park which

limits the further expansion of conifer forest, and promotes a policy of managing broadleaved woodlands.

The wilder open hills and moorlands are perfect for those who seek remoteness; but this remoteness can be dangerous when the weather can change so rapidly. There have been tragedies. Only experienced hill walkers should walk alone, especially in winter.

The busiest path is the Pennine Way which traverses the region from Greenhead on the Wall, to eventually climb The Cheviot before finishing at Kirk Yetholm over the border in Scotland. The Cheviot is an impressive sight, particularly in winter when the grass is bleached white. But its summit is a large wet plateau and one has to struggle around to get good views. Better prospects are from the heather-covered Harbottle Hills and the Simonside Hills, particularly the latter. Public footpaths also cater for the less intrepid walkers. Details of the programme of guided walks are available at the Park's information centres.

Northumberland National Park offers that feeling of an open wilderness; but somehow to me each fold of the hills has a statement to make. The Celts, the legions, the armies and the cattle robbers have all passed this way. In geological terms that was only yesterday. The landscape tells their story but has laid them to a silent rest, that stretches the understanding of the human role in nature, time and space. Each national park offers its unique sense of adventure; to me that is Northumberland's.

Hareshaw Linn in Hareshaw Dene. Deciduous woodland covers only 0.6 per cent of the park's land. The ancient oak and ash woods of Hareshaw Dene have been acquired by the Park Authority for protection. The ground flora is particularly rich.

The Broads

To someone brought up among hills, and who has worked and played amongst them since, the most surprising revelation on going into level country is the unrestricted view of sky. The hill walker is suddenly aware of it as he crests a summit, but it comes upon him gradually, and even then the sky on the horizon is usually obstructed by the convolutions of distant ranges. However, in a flat landscape one becomes inescapably aware of sky in all its moods, both during the day and at night with its vast legions of stars. Then, too, there is a new surprise as church towers and spires take on a special significance in the landscape.

The Broads is such a low-lying landscape, but one which offers great variety within its lakes and rivers, fens and marshes. Indeed, perhaps it should be called a 'national wetland' now that it has become a national park in all but name. While it is different from the other national parks, which are all in hill country, the Broads is none the less attractive and inviting for those who seek adventurous recreation in the outdoors; and from a natural history point of view it is extremely rich and vital – a huge area of wetland of international importance.

The area of the Broads extends around three rivers which meander over alluvial plains before reaching Great Yarmouth and the sea: the Bure in the north, served with its tributaries, the Ant and the Thurne; the River Yare from Norwich with its tributary, the Chet, and the River Waveney from beyond Bungay in the south. The broads, or lakes,

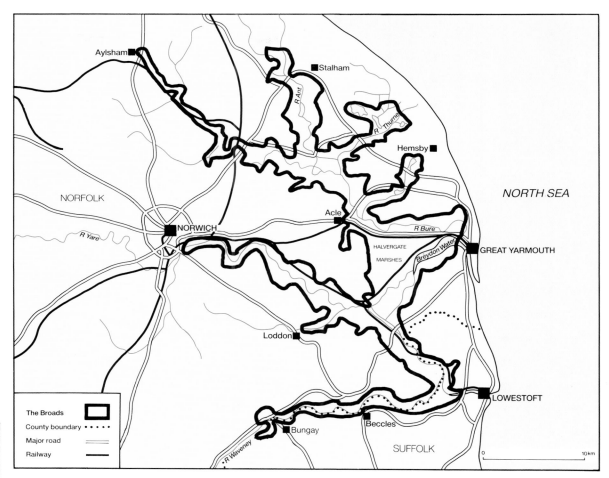

The Broads.

Year of designation	1988
Area	81 sq miles (210 sq km)

Natural areas of special interest

National Nature Reserves	3
Sites of Special Scientific Interest	24

Administering authority
Broads Authority,
Thomas Harvey House,
18 Colegate,
Norwich,
Norfolk,
NR3 1BQ
Tel: (0603) 610734
The Broads are mainly in the county of Norfolk, with a southern section in Suffolk.

Left:
A turf pond in Broads Fen. Turf ponds were formed by the flooding of shallow nineteenth century peat diggings, and now provide attractive habitats for a vitally interesting variety of plant communities. These ponds are one of the features which make the Broads unique in Britain and a wetland of international importance.

around these rivers are man-made sheets of water. In medieval times, vast quantities of peat were dug, down to thirteen feet or more. When sea levels began to rise in the thirteenth century, the pits became flooded and peat cutting was abandoned, apart from some shallow workings. These flooded peat pits provide the open waters which today are the forty-two broads. They were once more extensive than they are now, but over the centuries sediments and vegetation have encroached, gradually filling in the shallower lakes.

The broads lie within the flood plains of the rivers, which themselves provide more than 125 miles (200 km) of navigable, lock-free waterways. These

were important trade highways up to the nineteenth century when 'wherries' (large single-sail cargo boats) served the city of Norwich and the village 'staithes' (quays) on the river banks. When the Broads began to attract holiday-makers in the latter half of the last century, the gaily-painted wherries themselves were for hire. Although they provided very basic accommodation at first, later pleasure wherries and wherry yachts were more luxurious. It was between the wars this century, however, that the business of boat hire thrived and became the vital element in the local economy that it is today. Now more than 2,000 motor cruisers and yachts are available for hire, in addition to some 800 smaller vessels. However, a recent trend has been towards privately owned vessels; approximately a thousand are registered in the area. Twenty passenger vessels also operate in the Broads from a number of places, giving people the opportunity for 'park and ride' explorations.

In its natural state, the water in the broads has a rich, nicely-balanced aquatic vegetation with fish and animal communities, and has always attracted anglers. But the whole of the Broads environment – open water, reed bed, grazed marshland, fen and woodland – provides a rich wildlife habitat. Extensive areas are protected as Sites of Special Scientific Interest and as nature reserves, two of which (Hickling Broad and Bure Marshes) are also Ramsar sites, that is, they have been designated as wetland areas of international importance.

Hickling Broad, the largest and one of the most northern broads, is within a National Nature Reserve noted for its marshland birds, including two favourites of mine which live in the reeds – the acrobatic bearded tit and the shy water rail – and the extraordinary bittern which can stretch itself upwards to look like a bunch of reeds, with its legs acting as green stems, and whose spring 'booming' call carries for miles. The common reed, which grows to a man's height, has long been used as a thatching material. Hickling Broad, as in some other broads, still supplies the thatch needed for houses being built in other parts of Britain. Saw sedge, which is used to cap the ridges of thatched roofs, is also grown at Hickling Broad. Here too, in spring or possibly again in late summer, one might see Britain's largest butterfly, the swallowtail, which is the sole British member of the *Papilionidae*, a family which includes some of the world's largest and most handsome butterflies. The swallowtail caterpillar

Wind-pumps are another distinctive feature of the Broads landscape. At one time there were 240, but now only seventy-two survive and many are threatened by decay. Turf Fen wind-pump, illustrated here, is one of the seventeen renovated by the Norfolk Windmills Trust, aided by the Broads Authority in a continuing programme.

Opposite:
How Hill Nature Reserve, part of the estate which the Broads Authority purchased from the Norfolk Education Authority in 1983. The estate contains all the habitats and types of land use to be found in the Broads and an intensive work programme is bringing them back into management. The house and garden were purchased by the Norfolk Union Insurance group with the intention of setting up an environmental study centre. The How Hill Trust was formed in 1984 and the Broads Authority is working closely with it, organising courses, displays, and nature trails.

will only eat milk parsley, one of the scarcer umbellifers (cow parsleys and hemlocks) that grow in the fens.

Another National Nature Reserve is Bure Marshes, an extensive area down the Bure east of Wroxham at the point where the river is joined by the Ant. Here there is a variety of habitats covering open water, fen and alder carr (a marsh area which has become woodland). It includes the Hoveton Great and Decoy Broads, Ranworth Inner Broad and Cockshoot Broad. From Hoveton visitors can hire a boat to take them to a sleeper-path nature trail through a 'jungle' of the reserve's vegetation. Winter bird visitors here include wigeon, shoveller, pintail, tufted duck, goldeneye and smew; the pink-foot and white-fronted geese and the Bewick and whooper swans. Among the resident birds are the common tern and great crested grebe.

As well as a third National Nature Reserve, Ludham Marshes, there are a number of other reserves managed by the Broads Authority, the National Trust, the Royal Society for the Protection of Birds and the local conservation trusts: the Suffolk Wildlife Trust and the Norfolk Naturalists' Trust. The latter is one of the most active voluntary conservation groups in Britain and owns or manages many sites, including Surlingham Broad, south of Brundall, where the once-rare Cetti's warbler now breeds.

The animals of the Broads include several species of bat; the great bat, or noctule, flies like a swift and often lives in the hollows of pollarded trees. Coypus, South American water animals which escaped from captivity, once did extensive damage to river banks, but have now been eradicated from the area. Another escapee, the mink, is present in the Broads but has yet to cause problems. Two other less threatening animal escapees are the small muntjac deer and the Chinese water deer. Both are about the size of a whippet.

The list of plants found in these lush areas is also extensive. While the fen orchid is probably the rarest, the main attraction is the sheer luxuriance of vegetation in the Broads. But there are problems; nature reserves need management. If different varieties of species are to be encouraged then the dominant ones, such as the common reed, need to be harvested. Alder carr, if not managed, can quickly take over wet areas and, indeed, there has been a big increase in carr woodland since the war when management of the fens declined. (Alder

grows very rapidly in wet ground, and I remember, years ago when planting alders, my foreman warning me to stand back each time I stamped one in, or it would shoot up and knock off my cap!). Sallow and willow get away quickly, too, and the white willow can grow up to 80 ft (24 m) high. In the past it was sometimes pollarded to provide timber.

The problem is that much of the profit has gone out of Broads management, especially where labour-intensive tasks are involved. There is little to be made from cutting reed, sedge and marsh hay, although this *is* gradually becoming more viable in commercial terms. Carr timber was once cut and dykes were cleared when necessary to keep them open, but many are now silted up. The nature reserves rely heavily on the enthusiasm of active volunteers and people on government training schemes to help with management work.

But there are other serious problems. One is the

Cockshoot Dyke and Broad, part of a Norfolk Naturalists' Trust reserve. In 1982 it was suffering heavily from 'eutrophication' (over-enrichment by phosphates). After being permanently dammed off from the River Bure, thousands of cubic metres of enriched mud were suction-dredged away. Now the water is clear and typical aquatic plants have become re-established.

spreading 'eutrophication', or nutrient enrichment, of the water in the Broads which has been increasing steadily since the end of the nineteenth century. There are two main sources: phosphates from sewage effluent and nitrate 'run-off' from fertilised arable farm land, mostly from areas outside the Broads. Up to the 1960s, increased nutrients encouraged the growth of taller plant species in the broads and rivers, hindering navigation. Then the more advanced stages of eutrophication began with the water filling with algae, to the extent that it can resemble pea soup. The banks also suffer as they are eroded by the wash of passing boats in the upper and middle reaches of the rivers, a process which is not helped by geese grazing on the banks as they search for food.

As the years have gone by the situation has worsened alarmingly and there was seen to be a need for co-ordinated management of the Broads.

The Hobhouse Report of 1947 recommended that the Broads should be a national park, but this recommendation was not acted upon. Then the Nature Conservancy Council pressed for a strategic approach to management in 1965; this resulted in the formation of a Broadland Consortium which published a plan for the area in 1971. Still there was not enough action and seven years later the local councils, prompted by the Countryside Commission, set up the non-statutory Broads Authority. After an extensive review in the early 1980s, when a wide variety of organisations and local councils were consulted about the future of the Broads, the Countryside Commission was able to recommend that a special statutory authority should be established, and that the Broads should be given the status and central government funding accorded to national parks. The Norfolk and Suffolk Broads Bill enacted in 1988 finally achieved this status for the area; the Broads Authority will take on all its new responsibilities in April 1989.

Now the management of the Broads can at last be better co-ordinated and conservation efforts can be increased. The Water Authority is already taking steps to reduce the levels of phosphates in sewage effluent, and the Broads Authority has pumped out enriched mud from a number of broads. The problem caused by arable land run-off is being alleviated. An experimental scheme to encourage farmers to move away from arable cropping and revert to the traditional system of livestock farming on the grazing marshes was the forerunner for the establishment, by an EEC directive, of 'environmentally sensitive areas' where farmers can be paid to safeguard landscape and wildlife. All the Broads area has now been given this status.

However, it is early days and the Broads Authority has much to do. As well as being responsible for conserving and enhancing the natural beauty of the Broads, the Authority has to protect the interests of navigation in the area, which includes some of the most intensively-used inland waterways in Europe. The Authority also has to promote people's enjoyment of the Broads. There are already a number of nature trails, footpath guides, guided walks and visitor centres in the Broads, with the Authority working closely with other organisations in the area to co-ordinate advice and information.

In addition, the villages, towns and buildings which are part of the special character of the Broads need to be protected. Some are especially attractive: Ellingham Mill is an artist's joy, Beccles has fine Georgian houses, Bungay has its ancient castle ruins and Holy Trinity church with its eleventh century tower. There are many impressive churches, but the 'cathedral' of the Broads is St Helen's at Ranworth. It has a much admired rood screen but its treasure is the 'Sarum Antiphoner', an illuminated manuscript prepared by the monks of Langley Abbey in 1400.

There is little left of St Benet's Benedictine abbey which was founded early in the ninth century, but the site is still revered. Most of the walls of Burgh Castle, east of the junction of the Waveney and the Yare, are still standing. This was a Roman fort, part of their shore defences. It was used later by the Saxons, who built a monastery inside it, then the Normans who adapted the site as a motte and bailey stronghold.

Characteristic features of the area which command immediate attention are the 'windmills', which are actually wind-pumps used to drain agricultural land. Some of these are preserved by the Norfolk Windmills Trust, with full financial support from the Broads Authority within their area.

The Broads, where nature has enhanced what is man made, has everything going for it. The area is none the less welcome for attaining the protected status of a national park 30 years after the designation of the other parks. The Broads is indeed a vital part of our great heritage.

Postscript

I hope that it has been apparent from these pages that the national parks of England and Wales are special places that meet the urgent needs for refreshment, a sense of adventure, for recreation. They cannot be compared with national parks elsewhere in the world. On scale alone they could be dismissed. But beauty depends not upon magnitude, but on form and the harmony of forms – no violent contrasts but a subtle blending. And adventure does not necessarily require extremes of exertion and danger and distant journeys. It might be only one step away from normal routine to a new environment.

Wordsworth said of appreciating the countryside: '. . . it is upon the mind which a traveller brings with him that acquisitions, whether of pleasure or profit, must principally depend.' One must come to these national parks with no preconceptions, and a mind ready to experience a real appreciation of what, over the centuries, man and nature has achieved together. Then, perhaps, will be seen and felt a life-lasting love of the best of our countryside. There could be surprises. Some places are instantly warming, with no discordant elements, and offering the feeling that 'this is so, and could *only* be so.' But there are magnificent scenes too, that lack only fanfares of silver trumpets and choirs of angels.

What of the future? While being closely concerned with the social well-being of the parks' inhabitants, national park authorities should not think of their parks as 'country parks'. National parks need to be 'national'. There is a need to foster a publicly recognisable corporate identity which would encourage greater awareness and support for the parks. Problems, with thought and will, must be turned into opportunities. The landscape owes much to the stewardship of the hill farmers and a sustaining role must be found for them in the future policies of national parks. Broadleaved woodlands, groups of trees and hedges need to be restored for the enjoyment of future generations. One vital and considerable source of support – the enthusiasm of many volunteers – needs to be recognised and better cultivated. More power is needed by the park authorities to block damaging agricultural and forestry developments.

Lastly, and most important, much depends upon the government and its departments and agencies recognising and respecting the importance of national parks as vital rural assets that fit a fundamental public need; and resources should match that growing enthusiasm for informal recreation in an unspoilt countryside.

COUNTRYSIDE ACCESS CHARTER

Countryside COMMISSION

YOUR RIGHTS OF WAY ARE

Ω Public footpaths – on foot only. *Sometimes waymarked in yellow*

Ω Bridleways – on foot, horseback and pedal cycle. *Sometimes waymarked in blue*

Ω Byways (usually old roads), most 'Roads Used as Public Paths' and, of course, public roads – all traffic. *Use maps, signs and waymarks. Ordnance Survey Pathfinder and Landranger maps show most public rights of way.*

ON RIGHTS OF WAY YOU CAN

Ω Take a pram, pushchair or wheelchair if practicable

Ω Take a dog (on a lead or under close control)

Ω Take a short route round an illegal obstruction or remove it sufficiently to get past.

YOU HAVE A RIGHT TO GO FOR RECREATION TO

Ω Public parks and open spaces – on foot

Ω Most commons near older towns and cities – on foot and sometimes on horseback

Ω Private land where the owner has a formal agreement with the local authority.

IN ADDITION you can *use* by local or established *custom or consent,* but ask for advice if you're unsure:

Ω Many areas of open country like moorland, fell and coastal areas, especially those of the National Trust, and some commons

Ω Some woods and forests, especially those owned by the Forestry Commission

Ω Country parks and picnic sites

Ω Most beaches

Ω Towpaths on canals and rivers

Ω Some private paths and tracks. *Consent sometimes extends to riding horses and pedal cycles.*

FOR YOUR INFORMATION

Ω County and metropolitan district councils and London boroughs maintain and record rights of way, and register commons and village greens

Ω Obstructions, dangerous animals, harassment and misleading signs on rights of way are illegal and you should report them to the council

Ω Paths across fields can be ploughed; they must normally be reinstated within two weeks

Ω Landowners can require you to leave land to which you have no right of access

Ω Motor vehicles are normally permitted only on roads, byways and some 'Roads Used as Public Paths'

Ω Follow any local bylaws.

AND, WHEREVER YOU GO,
FOLLOW THE COUNTRY CODE

Enjoy the countryside and respect its life and work

Guard against all risk of fire

Fasten all gates

Keep your dogs under close control

Keep to public paths across farmland

Use gates and stiles to cross fences, hedges and walls

Leave livestock, crops and machinery alone

Take your litter home

Help to keep all water clean

Protect wildlife, plants and trees

Take special care on country roads

Make no unnecessary noise.

This Charter is for practical guidance in England and Wales only.

Further Reading

Countryside Commission official guidebooks
published by Webb and Bower/Michael Joseph:
Brecon Beacons by Roger Thomas
Dartmoor edited by John Weir
Exmoor by Glyn Court
Lake District by John Wyatt
Northumberland by Tony Hopkins
North York Moors by Ian Carstairs
Peak by Roland Smith
Pembrokeshire Coast by Herbert Williams
Snowdonia by Showell Styles
Yorkshire Dales by Tony Waltham

MacEwen, A and M *Greenprints for the
    countryside? The story of Britain's national parks*,
    Allen & Unwin, 1987
Redhead, Brian *The National Parks of England and
    Wales*, Oxford Illustrated Press, 1988

National Parks Today, newspaper published three
    times a year by the Countryside Commission on
    behalf of the national park authorities; available on
    free subscription basis from Countryside
    Commission Publications, 19/23 Albert Road,
    Manchester M19 2EQ.

In addition, all the national parks publish books and
    leaflets; contact each National Park Information
    Officer for a list of their publications.
Ordnance Survey/Automobile Association *Leisure
    Guides* cover many of the national parks, and
    include maps as well as walks.

Brecon Beacons

Barber, Christopher *Exploring the Brecon Beacons
    National Park (A walkers' guide)*, Regional
    Publications, 1981
Howell, Peter and Beazley, Elisabeth *Companion
    Guide to South Wales*, Collins, 1977
Mason, Edmund J *Portrait of the Brecon Beacons*,
    Robert Hale, 1975
Thomas, Roger *Journey through Wales*, Hamlyn,
    1986

Dartmoor

Crossing, W *Guide to Dartmoor* (1912), reissued, ed
    Brian Le Messurier, David and Charles, 1965
Gill, Crispin *Dartmoor: a new study*, David and
    Charles, 1970
Hemery, Eric *High Dartmoor: Land and People*,
    Robert Hale, 1984
Rowe, S A *Perambulation of Dartmoor*, (1848)
    reissued Devon Books, 1985

Exmoor

Enjoying Exmoor, Exmoor National Park Authority,
    1985
Blackmore, R D *Lorna Doone*, 1869
Burton, S H *Exmoor*, Robert Hale, 1984
Grinsell, L V *The Archaeology of Exmoor*, David
    and Charles, 1970

Lake District

Brunskill, R W *Vernacular Architecture of the Lake
    Counties*, Faber and Faber, 1974
avies, Hunter *The Good Guide to the Lakes*,
    Forster Davies, 1984

Millward, R and Robinson, A *The Lake District*, Eyre Methuen, 1974

Murdoch, J (ed) *The Lake District: a sort of national property*, Countryside Commission/Victoria & Albert Museum, 1986

Nicholson, N *The Lake District: an anthology*, Penguin, 1978

Rollinson, W *Life and Tradition in the Lake District*, Dalesman, 1981

Wainwright, A *A Pictorial Guide to the Lakeland Fells*, 8 vols, Westmorland Gazette, 1955–74

Wordsworth, William *Guide to the Lakes* (1910) reprint Oxford University Press, 1973

Northumberland

Charlton, Beryl *The Story of Redesdale*, Northumberland National Park, 1986

Newton, R *The Northumberland Landscape*, Hodder and Stoughton, 1972

Tomlinson, W W *A Comprehensive Guide to Northumberland*, Davis Books, 1985

White, J T *The Scottish Border and Northumberland*, Eyre Methuen, 1973

North York Moors

Atkinson, J C *Countryman on the Moors*, Ed J. G O'Leary, Oxford University Press, 1983

Hartley, M and Ingilby, J *Life in the Moorlands and North-East Yorkshire*, Dent, 1972

Mead, H *Inside the North York Moors*, David and Charles, 1978

Rhea, Nicholas *Portrait of the North York Moors*, Robert Hale, 1985

Peak

Bramwell, D *Archaeology in the Peak District*, Moorland, 1973

Dodd, A E and E M *Peakland Roads and Trackways*, Moorland, 1980

Edwards, K C *The Peak District*, Collins New Naturalist, 1962

Frost, R A *Birds of Derbyshire*, Moorland, 1978

Smith, Roland, *First and Last: the Peak National Park in words and pictures*, Peak Park Joint Planning Board, 1978

Pembrokeshire Coast

John, Brian *Pembrokeshire*, David and Charles, 1984

Lockley, R M *Pembrokeshire*, Robert Hale, nd

Miles, Dillwyn *Portrait of Pembrokeshire*, Robert Hale, 1984

Wright, C J *A Guide to the Pembrokeshire Coast Path*, Constable, 1986

Snowdonia

Breeze Jones, E and Thomas, G E *Birdwatching in Snowdonia*, John Jones, 1976

Condry, W *Exploring Wales*, Faber and Faber, 1970

Condry, W *Snowdonia*, David and Charles, 1987

Styles, S *The Mountains of North Wales*, Gollancz, 1973

Yorkshire Dales

Forder, J, Forder, E and Raistrick, A *Open Fell, Hidden Dale*, Frank Peters, 1985

Harrison, B and Hutton, B *Vernacular Houses in North Yorkshire and Cleveland*, John Donald, 1984

Raistrick, A *Malham and Malham Moor*, Dalesman, 1983

Waltham, Tony *Yorkshire Dales: Limestone country*, Constable, 1987

Wright, Geoffrey *Roads and Trackways of the Yorkshire Dales*, Moorland, 1985

Index